WISDOM AND TREASURES OF THE HOLY SPIRIT

Eleonore Prins

WESTBOW
P R E S S
A DIVISION OF THOMAS NELSON
& ZONDERVAN

Scriptures from the Holy Bible King James Version –
Tyndale House Publishers Inc. Wheaton, Illinois

Good News Bible – Catholic Bible
American Bible Society – 1865 Broadway, New York

Letter from Rev. Lloyd Williams from the Church of England
who participated in the Bermuda Triangle incident Prayers

WestBow Press books may be ordered through booksellers or by contacting:

WestBow Press
A Division of Thomas Nelson & Zondervan
1663 Liberty Drive
Bloomington, IN 47403
www.westbowpress.com
1 (866) 928-1240

ISBN: 978-1-4908-2398-0 (sc)
ISBN: 978-1-4908-4758-0 (e)
Library of Congress Control Number: 2014901435

Printed in the United States of America.

WestBow Press rev. date: 07/14/2014

CONTENTS

1. Hope and Wisdom 1
2. The Inner Voice 7
3. For He Will Give His Angels Charge over Thee★¹ 15
4. Dreams 24
5. I Go to Prepare a Place for You 33
6. Places of Interest 41
7. Star Wars 51
8. God's Purpose 64
9. Retreat 73
10. Prayer 83
11. The Holy Eucharist 91
12. The Light 102

HOPE AND WISDOM

———•◉•———

What is norm in one country is not the norm in another; therefore, this realm as such in any society is completely relative. There are many cultures and beliefs. What is kosher in England is out of the question in Thailand, so to speak. So normality in itself is quite relative. We have to adjust to the demands of the societies we live in, but we can always set our own standards in relation to our own lives in many ways. What is right for one individual is not acceptable to another, and so we have a very diversified world—especially here in the United States, where so many different cultures live side by side. Then, of course, the younger generation sets up its own principles; this is what each new generation has done throughout all the ages and centuries.

Nevertheless, when good values are to be thrown out for false or superficial standards, it is time to stand up and take notice and to bring about a change if possible. Also, when you hold on to a certain concept that displays the proper thought patterns in a certain culture, it could very well be based on a sheer matter of mediocrity or stupidity as a particular habit of thinking process passed along through the ages. Consequently, it is important to think things over and through carefully before one accepts or denounces certain matters, concepts, actions, and behaviors on the whole. Let us look at this culture of today. There are a lot of so-called Christians among us. However, many of them are surrogate Christians. We have a lot of imitation food on our supermarket shelves today; equally, we have a great many Christians who are also imitation versions on our shelves of the Christian echelons of today.

A senior citizen in the United States, for instance, is looked upon as a second-class citizen; so are women in some areas of the world, for that matter. However, concerning the elderly, this was not so in the old China; years ago, the old were always revered as the more knowledgeable ones—those who had acquired wisdom during their long journeys on this earth. Do the youth of today know better? No way. Just a few years' experience behind them might make them think that they are extremely streetwise, so to speak, and that is all they are unless deeper experiences have touched them since an early age in some way. Then there are those who have been fortunate enough to be touched by God at an early age or those who, through their difficult years and/or experiences, have acquired such a religious wisdom that their stories need to be told.

Then again, I also have had a long road behind me. I know that some of my years were full of golden treasures—not in the materialistic sense of the world. I have seen and been in many different countries in this world, and during these travels that were undertaken with a loving and caring family, much was given, and much was simply heaven-sent.

However, if and when a society forces one to fit into a square box, so to speak—a box of a collective mentality that suits a pagan-oriented culture and the media—it becomes suspect, especially when it tries to eliminate religion on the whole. But then, of course, there are a variety of religions. Some are traditional, and others are imbued with man's own thought of what religion should be and perhaps what would suit man's ideal. Unfortunately, churches often had to bow to the demands and pressures of this world, placing them in a weak position with no leadership of any kind, such as has happened in communist countries, those under fascism, or the former Nazi regime. Eliminating the true values of Christianity and placing them on a weak, little-meaning, and mediocre plateau is of no value or help to mankind.

Prayers have been removed from the schools. People with certain religious standards are withdrawn from leadership positions, and sometimes certain individuals are simply blacklisted from a particular group or cancelled in their roles on TV programs or intended lecture series elsewhere. All of this is because they do not fit that little square box that this society and the media have created for themselves.

Corruption on a large scale in the realms of business and this same type of bribery or fraudulent behavior on other levels in our industry have begun to accelerate on a regular basis. Indifference, careless behavior patterns in the business world and medical arena, and many different groups seem to be on the rise. When these behavior patterns are not dealt with, a country can go downhill. Much of it can also be as a result of a wrong sense of values, as we place too much emphasis on this life alone. We do not act in conjunction with the teachings of God.

There are other symbolic signs that are visible elsewhere. In the art world, for instance, the art being created today brings with it a shock value, and much of it can be ugly and lacking meaning. Kenneth Clark stated that "When a society, over a long period, produces an art which is lacking in vitality and imaginative power, but which nevertheless seems to be accepted by the majority, there is something wrong with that society."[*1]

Billy Graham, the well-known missionary, in his book *Angels, God's Secret Agents,* wrote about what he discussed when he was talking to Secretary of State Kissinger. He said that the world was experiencing an unseen war in which powers of darkness are attacking the forces of God and relates, "As we have moved through the turbulent events of past decades, I have become more convinced than ever that the activities of the unseen demonic forces are increasing."[*2]

We are part of a large universe; our small, earthly globe is only a fraction of the whole. When we shake our domains with false values and evil intent, it causes friction in God's setup for the normal balance of this universe.

I believe that the true Holy Spirit, being more aware of this than ever, is rattling his sables and urging us to be more aware, stand up, and speak up. Do I believe that Christianity and the Holy Spirit are relative? They are for real! "A rose is a rose as a rose is a rose" (Gertrude Stein); such are the actual facts. I believe that my writings verify the truth of this in every way.

There are those who are so close to God that they have been shown the realms of heaven and the continuation of the life hereafter. The late Agnes Sanford, healer, lecturer and wife of an Episcopalian minister, was one of these individuals, and her accounts are numerous in her books. Then there are those who have had such remarkable and beautiful holy experiences in their lives that it becomes vital for others to know and hear about them.

I felt it necessary to relate these experience of others and some of my own in this book so that those in this world can become aware also of what can take place— what is not being brought to light today and what can be done in order to make this a better world to live in. Then those who barely believe in Christianity and the holy order (as I call it) will try to better understand and begin to have genuine faith in God's purpose.

This book is in regard to seeing and understanding the religious scene and holy order from a difference angle entirely. It is like putting an altogether new disc into another drive in one's computer and viewing the world of the spiritual arena from the opposite end of a pole not yet contemplated much by the standards of society today. Those who have been enveloped in secular humanism and the superficial mentality of the group consciousness that this society has created for itself can find the ultimate and true values and concepts of the Christian faith in their own lives and futures today. They can realize and contemplate what is really at stake in and behind our lives today and reach for the blessings God had intended for them.

THE INNER VOICE

A n old, wise teacher of mine once said, "If we want peace of mind and a more secure and spiritual life, we should listen to the calling voice of God, who speaks to us constantly—but we don't listen!" In our materialistic and fast-paced society, in which one's hectic schedule and frivolous demands play a dominant role, it is not difficult to conceive that there is little or no time for prayer, and most important of all, to listen within. Anything and everything, including TV, seems to take precedence over the old concept related to a more contemplative or religious lifestyle. Since this is a forgotten pastime with no or little attention paid to its relevance, it has become a forgotten language, lost very far in an abyss of the unknown.

The element of importance in relation to listening within very often comes to the fore perhaps only for a moment when a problematic situation arises—something rather difficult to surmount, a grievous or perhaps an earth-shattering experience. In these instances, one will remember fleetingly that small voice within, way back, which will try once again to be acknowledged. If an inner urging is not heeded, the consequences can sometimes lead one's life into a wrong direction.

Sometimes, the small voice that you cannot hear but is simply an inner urging—an inner current, knowledgeable and directing—has been so squelched and neglected that it simply ceased to function. This is when one can suddenly be confronted with an insurmountable problem maneuvering into a state in which one is almost forced to come face-to-face with prayer and God's inner direction in order to steer life back into a sound, normal, and happy order.

I have learned through trial and error that if I don't listen within, so to speak, a wrong action or turn can be taken, and one can be confronted with its dire consequences. Its calamities are sometimes difficult to eradicate. Life's circumstances—the kind of situation in which an individual has to come to a halt—make one take stock and reevaluate his or her priorities in comparison to the priorities and standards of society and gear himself or herself more to the standards of the religious values taught. The final decision one has to make, in order to turn with the compass in the right direction, becomes the criteria. So it seems that one can be forced to listen for an answer, as one simply does not seem to appear on the horizon. This, in actuality, can be a wonderful turning point in one's life.

It can happen that one's life or circumstances can suddenly appear to have become nothing but a pile of rubble. Facing this dilemma—whether it is a loss of job and its years of dedication, loss of a family member, a relationship, or perhaps loss of goods, financial or otherwise, perhaps an illness within the family, whatever the cross one has to face—a change is demanded out of shear necessity, for there is no alternative. In reality, you can almost see the writing on the wall; God's hand has turned the tide. Even though at the moment, things can appear insurmountable and discouraging, one can begin anew, being given the opportunity to take time out to pray and listen within for the answer or direction.

No matter what predicament one is in, there is always an answer. Perhaps one's life is without any traumatic incident. It is still important to pray on a regular basis. An aunt and uncle of mine, both retired, have relied on this method prayer for years, and it has never failed them. They usually take time out for prayer after their 4:00 teatime. They have informed me that often, the element of surprise in reference to the direction given is amazing. For instance, one day, they were directed to call a distant relative as soon as possible, and as they did so, they found out that she was in urgent need of help from the family. The Holy Spirit is ever-guiding in all matters.

A friend of mine moved into an apartment building after she had had a strong inner urging (inner voice) not to do so. After the first year, she became aware of the reason she should not have made this move and realized that the elements she had to deal with in this particular place were extremely negative. It was not until about two years later that she realized that a move was imperative. If she had only listened to that inner urging, all of this could have been prevented.

I myself had a wonderful experience with this method of prayer. A startling example of the inner direction of the Holy Spirit came to me one day when I was out of a job. At that time, there were absolutely no prospects on the horizon. During my listening time one day, I was directed to call a firm that I had not been in touch with previously. Since I knew that jobs were extremely scarce in that corporation and a company not easy to get into, I dismissed it quickly and erased it from my mind. But then it kept coming back, repeatedly urging me to call *immediately*. I began to reprimand the Holy Spirit and said out loud that it was an absurd suggestion— ridiculous and totally out of the question. Nevertheless, I finally relented and called. The woman in the resource department simply said to me, "Can you come in for an interview right now?"

When I arrived at the company, I again mulled over the fact that this was quiet impossible and stopped worrying about the tests I had to go through and the protocol attached with these interviews. I did get the position on the spot, and when she gave me the approval, this woman in personnel said to me, "When you called this morning, I was sitting at my desk with this job order in my hands. I actually did not know how I was going to fill this one, as it demanded skills not easy to attain on such a short notice. When you called and told me about your background, I was quite sure that you would be perfect for this position." She also said that if I had called ten or fifteen minutes later, the job request would have already gone through a different route.

I stayed with that company for seven years, and it was the last job I had before retiring. It was also the best and happiest position I ever had.

What happens when you go against the inner voice? Another friend of mine was confronted with a bad decision in regard to this matter. She was engaged at the time to a man when God warned her inwardly several times not to marry this person. But she went against this warning and proceeded with the wedding anyhow. After several years of hardship in this sad relationship, the marriage ended in a divorce. She was made aware that those years were a dreadful waste and a deluge she caused herself as well as others who had been involved. All this was because she had not listened to that inner voice. It took quite some time and a lot of inner healing before she regained her equilibrium once again.

When I talk to family members who had been in precarious and dangerous situations during the war years, they have told me that their method of prayer and listening within often saved their lives. I have also been told that heads of state have saved countries from devastation with this method of prayer.

When attending a church or temple service, when we are aiming to be close to God, this is the time when the inner listening can be most important. Often this can be the time when God speaks to us through His quiet, inner voice in order to direct us or remind us of what should and can be done. It can be something that is unexpected or perhaps something that seems quite unattainable in our own estimation. However, if it is His will, we can be sure that it will be worked out along the way.

The Oxford Movement that was established in 1833 as a religious movement in the Church of England but founded by an American by the name of Frank Buchman advocated the teachings of prayer followed by the listening within in order to reach a closer unity with God. The movement came about when the reformation of the Church of England was at its height and the absolution and doctrine of baptismal regeneration was being dealt with. It was a time of seeking and a closer avowal of the sovereignty of God. The method of prayer and listening within of the Oxford Group was one of the finest that was ever established, and much can be learned from them even today.

"Our Lord speaks inside the soul without the din of words raising it up wholly to His divine love," said St. Ignatius Loyola. And the art of listening within can be rekindled if it has become a forgotten language in one's life. Very often, what the world, acquaintances, or friends want for us is not what God wants for us. The only way to find out what God's will holds for us is to learn to listen within. As children are often more in touch with the inner voice than the adult is, it is beneficial to remember the passage in the Bible that states, "Whosoever does not receive the Kingdom of God like a child will never enter it" (Luke 18:16–17).

You can start the art of listening within at a specific time—a quiet time before dinner, for instance, or after prayer time. Ask to be directed within. Or perhaps the mornings are more convenient—a time for prayer set aside early in the morning before going to work or starting the daily chores. At this time, it can be extremely instructive, as often, things can come up that we would have overlooked if we had not had a quiet time.

After the time of prayer, start the listening within for five or ten minutes at first. It will take discipline and determination. It is also necessary to keep a pad and pencil at hand and to write down whatever is given. At first, not much will be received unless you are an old hand at frequent prayer time. But with patience and practice, more will be understood of this fine and beautiful way of God to give us inner guidance and direction. These moments of dedication then can become longer as time progresses, and the results and blessings will begin to show their fruits as you proceed along this path.

The Bible speaks very vividly about listening to God the Father. Deuteronomy 28:1–3 says,

> And it shall come to pass, if thou shalt hearken diligently unto the voice of the Lord thy God, to observe and to do all his commandments which I command thee this day, that the Lord thy God will set thee on high above all nations of the earth: And all these blessings shall come until thee, and overtake thee, if thou shalt hearken unto the voice of the Lord thy God. Blessed shalt thou be in the city, and blessed shalt thou be in the field.

Henry J. M. Nouwen says, "The practice of a spiritual discipline makes us more sensitive to the small, gentle voice of God. The prophet Elijah did not encounter God in the mighty wind or in the earthquake or in the fire, but in the small voice (1 Kings 19:9–13)."

FOR HE WILL GIVE HIS ANGELS CHARGE OVER THEE*1

—•●✹●•—

Whenever I speak to a spiritual friend of mine who lives quite a distance away and I bid her good-bye on the phone, she always says to me, "I will ask the angels to be with you!" It is good to talk to someone who believes in angels.

We hear about the angels and read about them in the Bible. Books have been written about them, and art galleries contain the beautiful frescos and works of the old masters depicting these holy beings. However, in our fast and busy lifestyles, it is difficult to realize that there is an angelic existence, and not many believe or know that angels are actually there. When we grew up, we were told that we have guardian angels who are with us at all times. The church especially has given us this comfort and confirmation.

The Bible says that angel beings by nature are higher than man and closer to God. The angels receive more of His ideas, understanding, and light. Angelic rulers and angels learn all about God's secrets, powers, and wisdom in all its different forms (Ephesians 3:10). The more capable they are to oversee the many matters being constructed here on earth, the more equipped they are to help us. The ministry of angels is forever there to help us; this is clearly demonstrated in the Bible.

When Peter was in prison, an angel came to free him and broke his chains that bound him. Then the angel directed Peter to walk right past the guards to freedom (Acts 12:5–9). Other apostles were also released from prison cells. An angel strengthened Paul on a dangerous sea voyage, where he needed the help (Acts 27:14–25).

We do have guardian angels by our sides—sometimes several of them. But then there are three archangels whose authority has been everlasting. These are St. Michael the archangel and guardian angel of the Israelites. St. Michael is also regarded as the angel who leads the souls of the faithful departed to heaven.

Then we have St. Gabriel, the archangel who has been instrumental in a variety of communications. He delivered two important messages to Daniel (Daniel 8:25–27, 9:20–27). He also appeared to Zacharias to tell him that his wife, Elizabeth, would bear him three sons, one of which was John (Luke 1:5–20). He then delivered his most important message to the Virgin Mary and told her that she would soon become pregnant, and her child would be the Messiah. He said this would take place as she subjected her will to God (Luke 1:26–37).

St. Raphael was well-known for his actions in the book of Tobit. He helped in a situation where evil powers were at work and also was the traveling companion of Tobit. St. Raphael was also at work in Jerusalem and stirred the waters of a pool called Bethsaida. The waters were able to heal and restore (John 5:4).

The late Corrie ten Boom, well-known missionary from the Netherlands who was also imprisoned in the Nazi camps for some years, had an interesting experience after the war when she was on her way to deliver Bibles to Russia. Her suitcase was full of the books. Of course, the Scriptures were not wanted at that time in this communist country. When she got off her plane, she had to go through inspection and was quite anxious about how to get through these lines without her mission being detected. She prayed diligently to God to protect her case and for the books not to be detected by the custom officers.

She then suddenly saw the case totally surrounded by lighted beings and knew that these were angels. So when her turn came about and her suitcase was put on the table to be looked through, the officer commented that it was an extremely heavy case. But then, probably thinking that this elderly woman was carrying articles for the needy in Russia, he commented, "This is much too heavy for you to carry, and I will help you get it into the taxi," never opening or examining its contents. He helped Corrie take the case into the car and bid her good-bye.*2

Johnny Cash has related various confrontations with angels *(Man in White)*. When he was still in his teens, he saw a luminous being who told him that his beloved brother, Jack, would soon be taken to the other side. Two weeks later, he died in an accident.

After his father died, Johnny came home after the funeral. He was exhausted and grieving. He went to bed early, and in his dream, his father appeared to him as an angel. He related the dream:

> I was standing in front of my parents' house and a long bright car stopped at the curb. The rear door opened and my father got out and walked towards me. His clear eyes sparkled; they were not covered with the dull film of age I was used to seeing. His teeth were like a young man's and his hair was full and dark. A long light streamed between them. His father spoke and said, "Tell your mother that I could not come back. I am so happy where I am. I just don't belong here on earth anymore."*3

Billy Graham told a story about the Rev. John G. Paton, who was a pioneer missionary in the New Hebrides Islands. The missionary home was rather isolated on the island. One night, the hostile natives surrounded the compound, anxious to attack the missionary and his wife. The couple stayed up all night and prayed continuously. When daylight arrived, they were amazed that they no longer saw the troop of natives around the premises.

A few days later, the chief of the tribe converted to Christianity, and when the reverend asked him why the natives did not attack their home, he replied that it was impossible, because there was an army surrounding the house. He said that there were hundreds of big men in shining garments standing guard with drawn swords all around the mission grounds. The chief undoubtedly was quite impressed and thought that such an army would definitely be safe to have around.*4

A friend of mine who has the gift of discernment was on her way to a meeting. She had taken a shortcut in order to avoid the busy major highways and towns on her journey. As she was waiting for a red light on a rather small back street, she suddenly became aware of a group of angels of the holy order floating in and around the car. She wondered why and what purpose did they have to let her know that they were there.

When the light changed, she drove on and noticed that she was soon dealing with a legion of them and that they were totally infiltrating her car. Realizing that she would not be able to go much further, she stopped by the side of the road. Then she began to ask questions as to what this was all about. Was this a warning of some kind? But then she began to be aware that they were in a rather happy state, and there was no direct answer to her questions—only a jubilant type of mind and attitude and especially focused on the fact that there was no sorrow or grief connected with their mission. Being highly intuitive, she was also aware of some spirits accompanying this angelic group.

Slowly, they began to leave the car and continue on their journey. When she realized that they were gone, she finally started the car again and proceeded on the road once again. They had made it quite clear that this had been a mission of joy and not one of sorrow. As she drove down the road, she quickly noticed that from the opposite direction, a funeral brigade was coming toward her, and they drove by slowly. She realized then that the angels were there to take the individual home. There was a cemetery not far from there, and they had made a special effort to transmit to her their sense of jubilance.

My mother and father have been fortunate to have confrontations with the angelic. Compared to others, they lived very unusual lives. They were enterprising people, full of joy and a good sense of humor. They lived in the States but also lived for many years in Europe, Thailand, Singapore, and Indonesia. They usually spent their vacations in Europe, mostly France and the Netherlands.

It was on one of these trips to Europe that my parents had quite an unusual experience. They often liked to travel through the countryside, and while they were in France at this particular time, they wanted to make a point of visiting one of the older and beautiful cathedrals on their motor trip. It was a quiet time during the day in the early afternoon. No services or rehearsals were being held in the sanctuary. Few people seemed to be visiting this holy site, so they quietly walked through the various aisles of the church, admiring the lovely statues and artifacts. They had plenty of time and decided to make their way up the staircase to the different plateaus of this lovely, ancient structure. They passed several stalls that contained the different religious ornaments that were for sale.

When they reached the highest plateau, they went out to a balcony in order to take in the beautiful view of the countryside. Standing there quietly, they were suddenly aware of the most magnificent music they had ever heard—a choir with perfect and splendid tone, hundreds of voices, bringing forth a fine quality of music. My mother, who knew most the hymns and classical themes of the church, did not recognize the music; neither did my father. They looked at one another in amazement and realized that this was not coming from the church or any other earthly dwelling within the vicinity but from the heavens directly.

They remained there for quite a long time in wonder and awe until it finally disappeared. Being overwhelmed and in deep thought, they gradually made their way slowly down the stairway. When they reached the first stall, the nun behind the souvenir table, seeing the expressions on their faces, stopped them and said, "Ah, you have heard them. Yes, those are the choirs of angels of heaven; very, very few ever hear them up there on the roof when they come to visit this holy shrine. Wasn't it beautiful?"

A close friend of mine told me that she also had an unusual confrontation with the angelic world. When she was about ten years old, she went for a walk with her father in a rather isolated area. They often went for various walks in beautiful wooded areas near their home. When they reached a specific location, they sat down to rest for a while, and when they did, she suddenly heard in the distance music that seemed to come from a choir.

She thought at first that someone might have a radio, and she went to investigate the space around the particular spot they were in, but there was no one else around. She then noticed that it came from the heavens and that the music was exceptionally beautiful. As little as she was, she realized that it came from an angelic group. She said that she has never forgotten this amazing experience.

The second time my mother was confronted by the presence of angels was the day prior to my father's passing on to the other side. They were both sitting in the living room. My father had fallen asleep in his favorite chair while reading his newspaper. My mother was busy with some correspondence at her desk when she looked up from her work and suddenly saw three of the most beautiful angels standing around my father's chair. (My father, in his late sixties, was in comparatively good health.) The angels were looking down at him quietly.

My mother was aware of serenity and peace, and of course, she herself was startled and kept staring in complete disbelief. Then she noticed that the hair of these lighted beings was beautifully coiffured, each in a different style. Their clothes were light blue long gowns that seemed to be made of a lovely chiffon type of material. Their faces were kind and gentle. One of the angels looked up and saw that my mother was aware of their presence. She raised her eyebrows slightly and then smiled and nodded to her in a greeting. Soon thereafter, all three were slowly raised up and disappeared through the ceiling.

Early the following morning, my father passed away. Our whole house was permeated with a beautiful fragrance of flowers. There were no fresh flowers in the house. All who visited during that day and the following days commented on the exquisite smell of fresh flowers and asked where they were being kept. The angels had simply come to take my father home.

Some years thereafter, my mother was also taken to the other side. But she returned in a dream to tell me that she and my father were very happy. She also said to remember that God is extremely merciful, even though we doubt this at times. She said emphatically that she knew this to be true! We do have our resurrection in and through Christ, and He does give his angels charge over us.

DREAMS

————————•❋•————————

Dreams are God's silent messengers. They can warn you of a matter you might have overlooked or an action or thought that needs to be changed in your life. In today's fast-paced world, few take time to contemplate; most people are constantly on the run and have little time for inner listening. Nevertheless, God has a way to tap us on the shoulder in a dream and give His quiet direction or warning in order for us to change our actions, directions, or behaviors.

Psychologists have done a great deal of study in reference to dreams. They have been able to evaluate an individual's subconscious realms in relation to his or her life. Certain symbols, such as color, and apparently certain objects can be interpreted in a similar fashion. The well-known psychologists Freud, Alfred Adler, William Stekel, and Carl Jung established a Wednesday

Psychological Group in 1902. In this, they were able to compare notes on their theories. In time, it became the Vienna Psycho-analytical Society.

After a period of time, each one of these psychologists came up with his own conclusions concerning dreams and their interpretations. They evaluated that in one's own life, the symbols and dream recollections are extremely personal. Each symbol can be looked at in a variety of ways. However, according to Carl Jung, man has a basic "collective consciousness" in which certain symbols and colors remain and have the same meaning*.

Colors can have specific meanings in dreams. For instance, black would mean danger, the unknown, or hidden feelings. Blue meant openness, spirituality, or a blue mood. Brown meant earthiness and sometimes depression. Red meant danger—proceed with caution. Green meant positive change, a green light to move ahead, health, growth, and healing or sometimes jealousy, as green with envy. White meant peace, purity, and cleanliness. Yellow meant happiness, lightness, intelligence, or cowardice. Gold meant values—riches. The dream has to be looked at from all angles before one can determine what the meaning of these colors could be. But on the whole, it can be helpful in the interpretation of the dream in itself.

A good friend of mine had quite an unusual dream in relation to the man she was engaged to. Although this took place some years ago, she had broken her engagement to this man but was not able to get over the guilt and sad feelings she had. She kept wondering what was to be done. Then she dreamed that she was riding in a car with her fiancé. He was sitting in front, and she was sitting all by herself in the back. She would lean over to the front and say to him that she wanted to join him in the front of the car beside him. But each time, he would emphatically say, "No," she had to stay in the back. She kept up her pleading with him and even suggested that she might try to take the wheel now and then.

He became quite angry with her. Then she finally said that when he stopped at the next light, she wanted to get out of the car. So when he stopped at the light, she simply got out of the car, slammed the door behind her, and never looked back. This dream gave a symbolical and psychological explanation of what their relationship was really like and that in their life she would always have to be in a secondary position therefore it was not going to work out as things stood. After the dream, she no longer felt guilty and was actually quite relieved and then never looked back, so to speak. The problem was solved in a marvelous and practical manner.

A grandmother dreamed that she was very depressed, and when she looked out of her window, she saw a landscape that was flooded and dreary. She then recalled that someone said to her that her grandson had died. When she woke up from the dream, she was dreadfully upset. However, when she thought about the dream, it all appeared rather logical. She was depressed, because she hardly saw her grandson at all. He was so busy with the varied activities his parents had set up for him that he hardly had time for her as well. In her mind, he might as well have died, because he was never around to see her. She then decided to make the necessary changes in her life and make definite arrangements in order to get some special time with him in the future.

In the Bible, there are several passages that refer to the importance of dreams. The Lord spoke to Moses several times. However, Aaron, Moses' brother, and Miriam had been critical of Moses' actions. God requested through Moses that Aaron and Miriam be present when He came again during His next visitation. When they came together, the Lord came down in a cloud, and these were his words: "Should there be a prophet among you, in visions will I reveal myself to him: in dreams will I speak to him: not so with my servant Moses! Throughout my house he bears my trust: face-to-face I speak to him plainly and not in riddles" (Numbers 12:1–13).

Unfortunately, Miriam was punished by the Lord because of her indifference to God. But the plague that she was confronted with was removed from her some days later. What an incredible experience this must have been for these three people to have had the opportunity to be there in the presence of the Lord.

There are many accounts concerning dreams in the Bible. Dreams gave direction and altered people's lives. One of the most well-known dreams was given to St. Joseph. He had been planning to marry the Virgin Mary. However, when he heard that she was pregnant, he was planning to break the engagement to her. Then an angel of the Lord appeared to him in a dream and said, "Joseph, descendant of David, do not be afraid to take Mary to be your wife. For it is by the Holy Spirit that she has conceived. She will have a son and you will name him Jesus and he will save His people from their sins" (Matthew 1:20–21). This dream altered history.

There are other incidents in the Bible in which dreams played an important role in altering one's life. In the book of Daniel, Nebuchadnezzar dreamed dreams that troubled him. He kept seeing a figure made of various different elements. The figure was that of a man whose head was made of gold, a breast of silver, and a belly of brass, but the legs were made of iron and the feet part iron and part clay. None of his magicians could unravel the mystery of this dream. But then Daniel was told about it and had a vision of the interpretation of the dream. The king then summoned him.

When he appeared in front of the king, he said that the figure represented the various kingdoms that were to arise. The head of the man, which was made of gold, stood for the king himself, as his kingdom was full of glory and strength. However the others that were to follow were not of such high standards, and some would collapse as time went on. The King was so delighted with Daniel's explanation of the dream that he made him a great man and made him ruler over the whole province of Babylon and chief of the governors over all the wise men of Babylon.

Another important aspect of dreams is that they can be prophetic. They can relay a message of guidance to the individual who is dreaming. When I was a little girl, we lived in the Far East. All of our relatives were in the Netherlands, our actual home site. Just before

World War II, I had an unusual dream about my favorite aunt. War was certainly not on my mind; nevertheless, I dreamed that my Aunt Rieka and three of her sons were ordered out of her lovely home by a group of soldiers. They told her that she had only a few minutes to sort out what she could bring.

I saw a small cart on two wheels standing in front of the home, and then she and her boys quickly loaded it with some blankets, some dishes, and several bags. They were herded along with other people onto a street that ran parallel to their street. They all stood there along with other people who lived on the same street and watched their homes being blown up.

Later, after the war, she told us the story exactly as it had happened. The Nazis had led them out of their home, and they had only a few moments to take whatever was important to them and load it onto a little cart. Then they stood on another street that ran parallel to their home, an empty street, and watched their home being blown up. They lost all their belongings. War can bring dreadful tragedies. But my dream recorded the whole incident exactly as it occurred.

A beautiful dream came to me about two to three days after my mother had passed on to the other side. I was standing on a ledge, and suddenly, I saw Christ standing in front of me. His face was rather solemn but friendly. He said to me, "I am here in order to bring your mother to you, as she was so upset about the fact that she had not said good-bye to you, and she wanted to thank you for all you did for her." Then from the left side, my mother appeared.

She was walking slowly, with great difficulty, as she had done during the last years and was dressed still in her robe. There had been no alterations in her clothes or face. She came as she had appeared during the last stages of her life. She came and then kissed me and thanked me. I woke up soon thereafter, and instead of the intense grief I had felt, I was completely immersed with a feeling of ecstatic joy. Nothing like this had I ever experienced before, as it was connected with a religious affiliation.

This joy was immensely strong and real and. I knew that this incident had actually occurred and that Christ wanted me to know that she was with Him and that she had not made her transition as such at that time. That joyful feeling remained with me throughout the day along with a certainty about life after death and the care of Christ for us in every way. Those who leave this earth often have a message whish needs to be given and in our dreams they can communicate with us.

Sometimes God allows a family member who has passed on to warn a person of some event that is to take place. My mother, after she had passed on, often appeared in my dreams. She told me about the various stages one goes through after going to the other side, and she also warned me ahead of time about the death of a good friend of mine.

Not too long ago, I had been planning to spend some extra time with my special friend. We had set up various different excursions, as we are both artists. She had been ill and spent time in another state with relatives, and now she was better once again and had returned home. We were looking forward to this time, but then suddenly in a dream, my mother appeared and told me emphatically that my friend was not really well at all. She also warned me to stop planning ahead, as she said my friend would soon leave this earth plane and be with her on the other side.

I was devastated, as she was my best and oldest friend. Nevertheless, two weeks thereafter, my friend Margaret had a few small strokes. Soon thereafter, she lost her balance on the stairs and fell. She died instantly. (Her husband had died one week prior to this as well.) I was always grateful that I had been warned a few weeks ahead so that I could prepare myself for this terrible shock.

A coworker of mine had some interesting dreams in reference to her car. She dreamed the same dream about three times in a row. In each dream, she found herself driving her car. The vehicle would stall and then suddenly stop altogether on the side of the road. In one dream, the last one, she noticed that the headlights no longer worked and that she had to take the car to the garage in order for it to be repaired. Each time she told me about the dreams, she would explain that there was really nothing wrong with her car and that she did not understand it at all. Then she reasoned that it might be a warning of what was going to take place in the near future. However, when she thought about it further, she realized that she had been rather tired lately and then decided to see a physician about her own condition.

It was a good thing she did, as the physician found several difficulties pertaining to her own health. She discovered that if she had not gone for a checkup, her physical vehicle would not have been able to continue on the road. These dreams had been a warning to take herself to the doctor for a complete evaluation. The car represented her physical body and its function.

Abraham Lincoln, several weeks before he passed away, had a dream in which he saw that there was a coffin standing in one of the rooms in the White House. He was quite concerned about this. Some weeks thereafter, he attended a theatre performance and was shot. God had been trying to prepare him for his own death, which was to take place at that time, and did not give a warning to prevent it.

The interesting thing about your dreams is that you can keep a journal, and when you wake up, write down whatever you can remember about your nocturnal escapades. When you read them over, perhaps a few days later, the real meaning of these dreams you have recorded can give a clearer picture of what is taking place in your life. It might explain a psychological matter. Maybe you had overlooked something that was an important issue. Sometimes a warning can be of great value in this journey of ours.

The Bible stated that in Gibeon, the Lord himself appeared to King Solomon in a dream, and Solomon immediately inquired of Him how he was to handle a certain major problem he had been dealing with. The Lord then gave His instructions (1 Kings 3:5). God and dreams are great problem-solvers if we simply take the time to analyze the dreams and learn to listen.

I Go to Prepare a
Place for You

<hr/>

A distant relative of mine lost his wife some years ago, and his daughter, who has not been able to accept this loss, thinks that the spirit of the mother is still around. Many others who feel that they have to have some proof of survival turn to mediums in spiritualism or watch the TV shows where there seems to be comfort in hearing that the ones we loved are still floating around us.

All of this is a tremendous tragedy in itself—to think that God would allow such a depraved finality concerning our souls and spirits. I came from a family where we were steeped in the certainty and goodness of our beliefs in Christianity. My own mother had the unusual capacity to now and then perceive the realms of the other side. Sometimes spirits who were not taken up by Christ would appear to her. However, believers and Christians are usually taken to the realms God has prepared for them.

In the Bible, there are many affirmations about the continuation of our life after death. One of them speaks of it clearly: "For we know that if our earthly house of this tabernacle were dissolved, we have a building of God, a house not made with hands, eternal in the heavens" (2 Corinthians 5:1). Then there are many other statements given—one of them by Jesus: "In my Father's house are many mansions, I go to prepare a place for you" (John 14:2). This is very well-known.

There are many accounts of those who have had a life-after-death experience and have returned to tell about it. They all speak of the fact that we no longer remain on earth and that they have witnessed the trauma of a journey to the heavens where some have been able to see what God will have in store for one who passes on. Many speak about a strong light of God that sustains and carries them into these higher realms.

Betty Eadie, whose experiences were narrated in *Embraced by the Light,* spoke of the extensive journey to the outer spheres and then found herself in the presence of Christ. There was also a mention of those who were not taken up and stayed behind due to the fact that they were earthbound spirits who had not linked up with the holy order. They remain in a heavy tunnel of darkness— again, a realm outside of this earth plane.

The late Agnes Sanford, healer and author, had many visions of the heavens, diverse places, and realms similar to this earth plane (but more beautiful) where we will be when we pass on. She talks about this in her various books. She was married to an Episcopalian minister, and her many healings were truly miraculous. She writes, "But our real works, our creative accomplishments and activities of our spirit we will take with us to the heavenly realms (Rev. 14:13). He alone can know 'Eyes hath not seen nor ear heard, neither have entered into the heart of man the things which God hath prepared for them that love Him' (1 Cor. 2:9)."★1

My mother had two beautiful experiences that I want to write about, as they were very unique in themselves and proven to be true. When we lived in the Far East, we often traveled to the mountains for just a few vacation days in order to get away from the intense heat of the city. In these mountains, the air was cool and the lovely scenery comforting and restoring. My parents' schedules were extremely busy. My father's business was demanding and also took him out of the country many times. My mother's Red Cross duties and the many bazaars she set up in order to raise money for the different causes kept her always on the go.

She had also been occupied with helping a friend of hers whose daughter was suffering from cancer. The girl by the name of Hannie was extremely courageous and had lost her leg due to an accident. Cancer had set in, and the doctors predicted that she did not have long to live. The women bought her clothes and trinkets and took her wherever she wanted to go.

Anyhow, my parents had gone on their holiday in the mountains. One afternoon, while they were having their afternoon tea there, my mother suddenly saw Hannie's spirit appear in the doorway of the sitting room. The young woman appeared happy. She smiled at my mother and said she was saying good-bye, as she was leaving this earth plane now. My mother looked at her carefully and noticed that she was wearing a paisley printed dress with a rose flower motif on the fabric. The girl remained for a little while longer in the doorway and then disappeared quickly.

My mother immediately phoned her friends in the city, and the deeply grieved parents told her that Hannie had passed away just one hour ago. My mother related to them how the girl had appeared to her and then mentioned the fact that she was wearing the paisley print. My mother was acquainted with all of her clothes and said that she had never seen this particular dress before. Her friend then explained to her that this dress was a new gown just purchased the day prior to her passing and that they had decided to use this apparel for her burial, as it was such a lovely fabric. My mother had described the gown and its fabric completely and related perfectly the rose motif that was part of this print. My parents immediately returned to the city in order to be with the bereaved parents.

A friend of mine told me a very unusual story not too long ago. She had a phone call from her niece in Chicago, and she related to her that a friend of hers who had been a jogger with her for several years had suddenly died. But the gist of the story was quite surprising. During the previous week, she had been jogging with this male friend as usual, meeting on the specific street corner at the same time as she had done for some years. However, that particular morning, they had met, and he had not been too talkative. As they parted, he said good-bye and stated that he would not be seeing her for a while, as he was being relocated and was looking forward to the transition. Before she could ask him any further questions, he had already walked away. She thought it was all very strange to leave her so uninformed while they had been such good friends.

After she got home, a friend called and told her that her jogger friend had passed away during the night. The niece then said that that was impossible, as she had just jogged with him for one whole hour, but that he had acted strangely at the end and told her what had happened. But all the evidence was there. He had passed away during that night. He undoubtedly wanted to bid his jogging companion good-bye and obviously knew where he was going.

On December 20, 1943, Private George Ritchie died of double lobar pneumonia. What happened to him when he passed on to the other side was quite a revelation. George was on his way to Richmond, Virginia in order to enter medical school. However, during mid-December, he had suddenly become extremely ill and entered the hospital near camp Berkeley, Texas. Then he unexpectedly died on December 20 during that year. What happened to him was an incredible experience— one he would never forget.

When George died, he remembered that he stepped out of his body. He had been so anxious to enter the medical school that all he could think about was that he had to get to the station to get the train to Richmond for his medical training. However, when he walked down the hospital corridor, he noticed that everyone he spoke to was totally unaware of him and that they were walking right through him, as he had no substance or body at that time. They ignored him completely.

He realized then that he was in a different dimension and did not have a body any longer. He quickly ran back to his room and then found his body where he was still lying on the bed with a sheet draped over him. Although he was covered, he recognized that it was him, as his hand with his fraternity ring was lying beside the sheet.

As he contemplated his ordeal, there was suddenly an extremely bright light that he knew was the presence of Christ. He heard within himself a voice that said that he was standing in the presence of the Son of God. The room became flooded with light and a strong feeling of love. He knew then that he was standing in the presence of Christ himself. Quickly within that light, he was then shown a series of pictures, and they were events of his life. He became clearly aware that it had been so far a trivial and irrelevant existence. The question came to him, "Did you tell anyone about me?" No, he really did not think much about that.

Suddenly, the light changed, and he seemed to enter into this world that he was in, but it was shown that there were persons all around who had died and were in a state of grief and despondency. Each individual was occupied with earthly things and not getting or receiving any gratification. They were wandering around aimlessly, trying to talk to the living, who were not aware of them at all. They were the souls who had apparently not thought much about God or Christ in any way when they had been alive. He realized that he did not fit into that category.

He was then permitted to see two other worlds. The first one appeared more real and solid than the world we live in on this earth. This other world had a new quality of light and openness of vision, but it was a better world—one in which there was a centeredness of truth. He saw composers, sculptors, universities, and great libraries and scientific laboratories. It was a genuinely productive and beautiful world.

But then, suddenly and quickly, he seemed to be transported into a world that was very far away, and there he could see a city constructed out of light. At that time, he had not read the book of Revelation or had anything to do with the afterlife. But this beautiful and great city that he could see was made of houses, streets, and walls that emanated light. Then he also saw beings who themselves were embodied in light, exactly like Christ, who was standing beside him. This vision seemed to be a short one, as he was then again shown the little room in which his body was lying on a hospital bed. As he looked at his own body lying there, a strange and deep sleep came over him.

Private George Ritchie had been escorted back into his body. The doctors examined him when he awoke and said that it was a miracle that there had not been any brain damage. A soldier had been assigned to prepare him for the morgue, and as he did so, he became aware that his body had shown some form of life. He quickly called the doctors, and they immediately gave him a shot of adrenaline into the heart.

Later on in life, George made this statement:

> Today I feel that I know why I had the chance to return
> to this life. It was to become a physician so that I could
> learn about man and then serve God. And every time
> I have been able to serve our God by helping some
> brokenhearted adult, treating some injured child or
> counseling some teenager, then deep within I have felt
> He was there beside me again.*2

God undoubtedly has prepared a place for us after
life—and not one on this earth, wandering around
without a body unless we have negated our trust in
God and His teachings. Holding on to the spirit world
is not what God or Christ had intended for us to do. To
seek the holy order and will of God is our true vocation.
This is the very reason we came upon this earth to begin
with. Our lives are short and fragile, and one can only
handle life with the utmost of care. God calls us to be of
service to Him, and if this is done, we undoubtedly will
go to the place that has been prepared for us.

PLACES OF INTEREST

———————•❋•———————

Territories seem to hold and maintain the incidents and actions that have taken place in that particular area. When an area is so influenced by a particular action, many times with charged emotions having taken place in a definite location, the atmosphere then is imbued with the molecules and memory of such phenomena. I always say that not in the too distant future that physicists will be able to measure these realms with certain instruments to prove their point. Nevertheless, the spirit of discernment is able to evaluate some of these areas and bring about the needed change.

Genesis 4:8–10 states that Cain and Abel, the two brothers, had a severe quarrel. As a result, Cain killed his brother, Abel. This dispute and its detrimental violence caught the attention of the holy order, and God cried out to Cain, "Where is your brother, Abel?" And Cain answered, "I don't know. Am I supposed to take care of my brother?" Then the Lord said, "Why have you done this terrible thing? Your brother's blood is crying out to me from the ground, like a voice calling for revenge." Cain was punished by God for this and was not able to grow any crops on the land. The grievous circumstances permeated the ground and air and would remain as such.

When I was about ten years old, we lived in a large, old house situated among some beautiful hills and ravines near a town in the Dutch East Indies. The house had a large garden, but at the end of the backyard, there was a hedge that separated the property from the hills and ravine areas surrounding the territory. As children, we had discovered that behind the hedge, on the other side, facing the ravines, was a small path leading its way along the partition. When you stood on that path, you overlooked a huge drop on that side into the ravines below.

These ravines contained smaller hills and some rice paddies, all of which were an incredibly beautiful sight to behold. With my adventurous spirit and some good friends, I had already taken that little path along the hedge and further along its mysterious winding road and had found a terrace situated at the end of this little roadway. We loved going into those forbidden places where no one could find us.

This terrace or ledge at the end of the pathway contained the necessary equipment to make oneself comfortable. There was a bench and a small table, and the lovely foliage surrounding this little seating area made it a cozy little getaway. As children, we liked such adventures. Whenever possible, we would be on our way along these different hills and pathways in and among the ravines and hills.

However, I soon noticed that that particular terrace, with its romantic panorama, always held an incredibly heavy and tragic atmosphere. This in itself took away much from this beautiful spot. It was not until later, before we moved away, that I learned that lovers had taken their lives on that little terrace, perhaps due to circumstances in which there seemed to be no other way out for them. The natives on these islands were of various different religions, and many did not intermarry into faiths that had not been part of their families and ancestors. The ground here was also calling out to the Lord.

It seemed that the Far East and its luscious islands were the place to go. In Europe, it was assumed that in the Far East, one could make a whole new life for oneself and family. Financially, the prospects were very good. So consequently, many came and stayed until it was time to retire, and then they would return to Europe once again, whether they were German, English, Belgian, French, or Dutch. At the time of retirement, they would return home in order to settle down in their own homeland.

My mother and father's families both came out to explore the areas. Aunts and uncles, with children or without, came out. Some went back quickly, not being able to adjust to a new and strange culture, and others stayed in order to find a new life. This new culture certainly was something one had to adjust to, as some of its practices were rather bizarre.

One of my aunts, with her husband and two sons, had purchased a lovely new home. This home, with about another twenty, had been built on a new tract of land. As it is the custom in the Far East, one usually had several servants. She had about four of them. She had been terribly enthusiastic about the new home. It seemed that it contained all the new features one could expect in such residences.

The family moved in and then noticed that during the first week, the house began to rattle strangely during the night. But then during the second week, one day at noontime, they suddenly heard an incredibly loud noise on the roof. When they ran outside, they saw to their astonishment that stones of all sizes were coming straight down from the sky and falling on the roof. The phenomena began to take place each and every day just around noon. But this was also happening to the other new homes down the street. It was almost unbelievable.

The servants resolutely left after that first week, and as this strange occurrence kept repeating itself, every one of these homes was soon vacated. After further investigation, they found out that the houses had been built on top of a Chinese cemetery and that there had been a great dispute among the locals and those who had ancestors in these plots concerning the building of new homes on this particular land.

With my mother, I lived in England for some years. When we came back, we settled back in the States, although in a quaint and attractive historical area. George Washington and his troops had resided there, a place in which many strategic battles had been fought and many plans for the future had been organized. Whenever I walked within and near the old compounds where the military troops had been stationed, much was still lingering around.

Soldiers who were heavily wounded and injured and undoubtedly had no religious affiliations had died within these territories. There had been a hospital for them on these premises, and I could pick up the tremendous suffering that had taken place. It was known that at the time of these battles, they had had an extremely strong winter. Heavy snows enfolded all the areas where these troops were stationed, making things undoubtedly much more difficult. All of their dwellings and materials were terribly primitive at that time. The whole entire area surrounding the old town was infested with the memory of lost souls of the troops who had died there.

When an area is imbued with the long-lost memories of war battles and sometimes the souls who have not found rest during that time, the territory is enfolded in a realm of actual darkness, sadness, and a strange and strong sense of depression. Such was definitely the case here.

Some months later, after having moved into this historical area, a minister friend from the UK happened to be traveling through this location. When he arrived, he asked if I had encountered anything out of the ordinary within these locations. He frequently cleared the many sites in Europe and has excellent discernment in reference to these realms.

I took him into the areas where these soldiers of George Washington had rested and lodged. He immediately became aware of the remnants left behind from that war. He said that there was absolutely no doubt in his mind that all of this had remained for many years. We prayed at the sites, and then Rev. Steven Kyle conducted a service for them and a special Holy Communion for the lost souls the following evening at the church. Since this took place, there have been no further sightings or remnants that we have encountered in and around these historical places or in any other locations around the old town itself.

Rev. Steven Kyle, a minister of the Church of England, conducted the Holy Communion for these lost souls at the Convent of St. John The Baptist in Mendham, New Jersey, and the following is his statement in regard to the George Washington troops:

> I was very pleased to hear from you the positive results of our collaborative efforts regarding the souls of the deceased soldiers caught up in the drama and dynamics of old Morristown. These soldiers had died in struggle, many with no faith in God and most unable to make a confession prior to death. Upon death, they had not been able to travel on toward heaven and had remained stuck for centuries, waiting for help, for prayers offered in the name of Jesus, who alone does marvelous things and many miracles. Reverend Steven Kyle

Another area that held the actions of the past in limbo was an old church out in the country. I had started to attend this quaint, old little Christian establishment that was situated on a large hill; it was considered a high

Episcopalian church. However, during the first weeks when I was there, I soon became aware of the presence of animal spirits that seemed to be filling the atmosphere of this old building whenever there was a Sunday service in progress. Even though the Holy Eucharist brought in the holy presence, these entities were continuously there.

When I told the minister about this, he immediately acknowledged the fact that this had been so and related that the bishop had also been aware of them. He told me that they had a service in regard to this phenomenon and had prayed over them various times, but apparently, the animal spirits had no intention of leaving the area. I thought it was best to investigate further. I went to the library and found some books on the history of that particular vicinity, and they revealed a great deal. The books were quite informative about this old territory.

The Lenape Indians apparently had inhabited this part of the old wooded New Jersey landscape and had been there for quite some time. They were a very peaceful tribe but with specific customs in relation to their religious rites. One of these was in regard to the sacrifices of animals during their religious ceremonies, and all of these rites were always performed on a hilltop. This top of the hill had apparently been used for these ceremonies for centuries and prior to the appearance of this church.

The pastor of the church then performed a Holy Eucharist in the wooded section behind the building, where he thought that most likely, these rites had taken place. Not long thereafter, the grounds were clear, and so was the church. There were no longer any animal spirits floating around the place, as they had been taken up. The church now stands triumphantly on that hill, and its congregation is flourishing.

Archeological circumstances can have a specific effect on certain sites in a variety of ways. A friend of mine was living in a particular apartment building with all the conveniences and fixtures one can think of, making it especially comfortable and agreeable. Nevertheless, all through the building and surrounding areas, there was a definite, depressing, and gloomy atmosphere. Visitors had commented on this on several occasions. Then an acquaintance stopped in one day. She had the gift of discernment and mentioned to her that on one of the walkways outside of the building, she had discovered a magical ring of some kind. In England, these are quite common and have dated back to the Druids and Stonehenge. But in the States, they are not common in that respect.

The church came to the rescue, and after further investigation and historical research in the library concerning the grounds, it seemed that a certain tribe of Native Americans had inhabited the lands. A Eucharist in regard to the historical facts and magical rites was done, and not too long thereafter, the whole aspect of the morose atmosphere within the building soon disappeared.

The well-known late Dr. Kenneth McAll, missionary, physician, and psychiatrist from England, often visited the United States. He and his group had many experiences in regard to clearing the various important locations in Britain.

In the States, he liked to go to the different sites where the Native Americans were buried and pray and clear all of these old burial grounds. The Native Americans did not always appreciate much of this, as they often used those grounds in order to pray and communicate with their ancestors. Their ceremonies were very much in relation to this particular practice. Nevertheless, Dr. McAll, while on his vacation in Idaho, visited a dude ranch. There he and his group took part in a peace pipe ceremony. The intention was to help those who had passed on to be released from this earthly plane.

A lady present in the group who had the gift of discernment said, "Who are all of these people standing around and about the circle?" Dr. McAll told her that they were the deceased Native Americans who had lived there and that he had asked Jesus to take them up during the Holy Eucharist that was to follow the Native American ceremony. This all took part with great reverence, and when the services had taken place, he said that over five hundred of them had been taken up that day. ★

In England, the priests clear the cemeteries. This is quite a common practice. The earth and ground in which a loved one has been buried and the surrounding areas often contain the grief of those left behind as well as energies and entities that are not of the holy order. All of this roams around, and these realms need to be cleared and healed of their torment and memory.

The blessings of the earth are very important. I remember well that while I was living in London, one afternoon, I spent some time with a friend. We had gone into one of the smaller parks or mews in back of a residential district and were sitting in a well-tended and lovely rose garden. It was adjoined to a communal garden, where there were numerous small plots containing the vegetable gardens of the residents of that particular area. Behind those communal plots, there was a small cemetery.

The day was full of sunshine and the air full of sparkle when I suddenly noticed a priest who was walking among the two gardens and just finishing his blessings and clearing of the cemetery moving into the vegetable garden. I could hear him saying the spiritual blessings, and I could see his white robe swirling around him while he was sprinkling the gardens with his wand and holy water. He was turning from left to right, and I could see the joy in his face while he was in the midst of this beautiful prayer vigil. No wonder these gardens looked so well-kept and prosperous; they were receiving God's blessings on them weekly. I could feel the joy of God's great handiwork and love.

STAR WARS

—•◉•—

S
tar Wars and its fabulous stage effects on the screen have made a terrific impact on society, especially the young. Spaceships zooming from earth to outer space among different planets are quite thrilling. But star wars actually are very much a part of our lives each and every day, but on an entirely different level. In order to get a glimpse of what I am talking about, I will explain it from various perspectives and angles. Whether it is as colorful and exciting as on the screen is according with one's own evaluation, understanding, spiritual development, and discernment.

There is a well-known passage in the Bible that states, "We do not fight against flesh and blood, but against the wicked spiritual forces in the heavenly world, the rulers, authorities, and cosmic powers of this dark age" (Ephesians 6:12). Yes, all of these forces here on earth and the other forces that abide on the other side.

Whenever I say anything about the principalities and dominions, not many seem to understand what this is all about. Light comes from above, but so do the dominions and principalities.

These principalities and dominions play a role in our lives and our very existence. They are part and parcel of this universe and very active in their particular roles. Those who have the discernment of the Holy Spirit are much aware of these realms. We are not walking within unchartered waters. The first time I became aware and was introduced to these phenomena was when I was still in my early teens.

During my early years, we lived in the Far East, and we had a total of about twelve servants, sometimes more because of the various tasks included due to the specific holidays and times of the year. I remember well that on the major holidays, like Christmas and Easter, there was always a pageant of the servants. On the major holidays, the servants would come to greet my parents and wish them blessings for the special holy days involved. Each one of these natives would come all dressed in his or her Sunday best and stand in line in order to make a special and honorable presentation toward their employer. This, for them, was definitely a regal occasion and regarded with great reverence. However, this special event would take an enormously long and tedious time in order for them to accomplish this feat.

It is interesting that all these servants were from a variety of religious backgrounds. Some were Hindu and some Muslim; others were Buddhist or Shinto, and some had no affiliation at all. They also came from different regions of the islands. Some were not from Indonesia but from the Malaysian continents or the Chinese borders. They had great respect for their own religions but also had respect for the Christian employer as well, and this had to be demonstrated in a beautiful and specific manner. In the Far East, one's manners and customs were of great importance.

As they would stand there in their splendid outfits, I would have a long time to observe these extraordinary people in their magnificent costumes from all angles. I would sit in a little chair, taking in all this spectacular entourage. It took some hours, because each and every one of them would present a gift and a speech. The colors and lovely lines of their clothes would capture my interest at first, but then I began to realize and be aware that each and every one of these people had a realm, so to speak, standing behind him or her.

I was very young, and the Holy Spirit was showing me then that these people were not standing alone but that a dominion of some kind seemed to stand behind them. At this early age, it was difficult for me to interpret or define the meaning of this, especially as these servants came from such different religious backgrounds. But somehow, I realized that these realms behind them were not only part of them, but also had an existence of their own!

It was not until years later, after I had received the Holy Spirit again, that I understood how these realms were related to an individual. I understood more specifically what these so-called dominions or principalities were all about. But at that young age in the Far East, it merely seemed like an energy force consisting of its own and yet part of each and every one of these charming individuals. I did not know then what these dominions were; to me, these were merely a mystery all of their own, and they created a sphere somewhere behind each one of these individuals.

Later in years, I began to be aware of these dominions on a regular basis. One of the gifts of the Holy Spirit is the gift of discernment of spirits. In my case, the Holy Spirit gave me the gift to detect the principalities that are behind the spirits. It all consists of the awareness of what is in existence on the other side. Many times, I do know what realm or principality is involved, but at other times, I do not know. Then the Holy Spirit, on each occasion, can always detect the realms that are present at a certain time.

I remember an interesting incident I experienced one summer when I was helping out at a well-known college. I was on my way to the computer room and entered an elevator to go to another level. A charming black woman entered the elevator; she was holding a black suitcase. She seemed a kind individual and greeted me as she walked in. I noticed that she was well-dressed, although quite conservatively.

I then became keenly aware of her surroundings, as we were on the elevator alone; this was not hard to do. But the fact that held my interest was that she was completely surrounded by the realm of the holy order—actually, a strong dominion of the Christian order. Not many have this privilege. I wondered if she was a minister or taking her studies to become part of the clergy in the Christian church.

Nevertheless, my stay in the computer room came to an end in the later part of the afternoon. I then made my way back to the elevator. Surprisingly, the lady who had been my companion before also showed up and entered the elevator with me once again. We exchanged some comments, and I immediately became aware of the intense presence of the principality of the woman's ancestry. The African order was heavily imbued around her. Although the holy order had been easily detected previously, the ancestral control and dominion made their strong and heavy presences known. It seemed to me then that we can't dissipate the dominions of our heredity entirely.

A close friend of mine who passed on to the other side not long ago seemed to be part of an interesting phenomenon as well. She was a good Christian and had a great sense of humor but always held on to the traditions the church had taught her. Just the same, it was quite often that I was aware of the pagan realms that seemed to surround her so strongly. When we talked about it, she always remarked that her ancestry was not in the least bit interested in Christianity, and she was hoping to make a further study of their lives when she could find the time. She was a student of archeology, taking night courses to obtain her degree, working full-time and bringing up a son as a single parent.

Some time ago, I was attending a prayer group that focused primarily on finding new employment. Jobs were scarce then, and many had been let go.

Consequently, this prayer group had been set up in one of the churches, and it certainly was extremely beneficial. The leader was a Christian minister. He had a great deal of knowledge on how we would find and go about getting other jobs.

Each time I was there, I became aware of the Christian realm around this leader, but I also was aware that he had a strong Jewish dominion somewhere in the background. One day, while talking to his wife, I tried to find out more about him. She told me that her husband was originally from a Jewish background and had been a rabbi before he became a Christian minister. It seemed that there was no conflict between these dominions, and he was able to be a great leader in his church and a happy provider for his family. Nevertheless, the Jewish dominion had no intention of disappearing from the scene and seemed to hold on tenaciously at all times.

Now these principalities and dominions that are navigating in and around an individual are certainly part and parcel of the bloodlines and ancestry. However, there is more on the horizon line that some who are on a higher spiritual level are keenly aware of. These are in relation to the dominions that operate and control not only certain individual levels, but also nations, churches, corporations, areas, etc. and are undoubtedly the invisible forces that control our human existence to a certain extent. As Walter Wink explains it so avidly in his book *Unmasking the Powers,* "The old gods of paganism are still very much alive and the denial of this fact only guarantees their repression." But this is only on the outward level.*1

In Daniel 10, we read that Daniel was terribly dismayed due to the fact that his prayers had not been answered. No matter how hard he prayed, he thought his pleadings had not been heard. But then an angel appeared to him who told him that help from God was on its way but that it had been fiercely blocked by the angel of Persia. The holy angel then obtained the help of St. Michael, the archangel of Israel, in order to reach Daniel. Just the same, this in itself did not alter things, as he still had to fight the realms of the angel of Greece thereafter. The deities and angels and their dominions apparently have power to control and obstruct the realms and various sections and again are allowed to do so for certain periods of time.

Ephesians 6:10–12 explains it all. I would like to repeat this once again.

> Finally, my brethren, be strong in the Lord, and in the power of his might. Put on the whole Armour of God, that ye may be able to stand against the wiles of the devil. For we wrestle not against flesh and blood, but against principalities, against powers, against the rulers of the darkness of this world, against spiritual wickedness in high places.

The powers and these dominions then can fight to hold God's messengers at bay. These treacherous wars in heaven undoubtedly take place at random and have done so for centuries. Walter Wink explained in his book that the intense strongholds here on earth are ever exerting their power, and these continue to control much of this world. When we think that these powers and so-called angels (some fallen), deities, or controls actually reign over nations, churches, institutions, and a variety of areas, and that we are forever under the banner of their manipulations...................

Yes, the pagan gods are very much alive today in the many groups and concepts of society. The dominions and principalities are very connected to this earth and the lives of people here and now. They are connected in the outer atmosphere, where they wheel and deal their intended actions, sometimes clashing and combating against other opposing realms and especially those of the Christian sector. When this occurs, we have the clashing of star wars with the combustion of the light ranges far and wide. The frequency of light is certainly varied in this respect, and the color clashes along with it. If we could see this spectacle, it would be like the fireworks of July 4. Perhaps we will be able to see this someday in a most marvelous way.

Even corporations have their controlling powers. When we look at Enron and the other institutions that have had their fraudulent practices exposed, it is a fact that cannot be ignored. Wink questions the matter that a nation such as Germany could have allowed a Hitler to have taken charge on such a large scale. What if the churches could have taken a stronger stand against the demonic stronghold that occurred through the Nazi regime? This demonic takeover of the collective consciousness of a whole nation undoubtedly in and through the realms of the satanic dominions was not halted by the holy order until later. This holocaust caused the loss and devastation of the millions who died and suffered during that time.

If mankind had been more spiritually advanced, perhaps all of this could have been averted, and the demonic realms that took over a whole nation (plans for the whole world) could have been avoided and defeated before they took root. But the Christian concepts and churches were trampled down and negated in this German nation by the forces of evil for a limited time only. It took World War II and millions of lives and prayers to eradicate them.

Some who live on a higher plateau can detect the angels and controls of the nations, states, corporations, churches, institutions, and various areas. They can see and be aware of those who sit behind the scenes and are in the driver's seat. And then we come back to one of the major issues—the principalities we bring along from ancestry, the pagan realms that undoubtedly unite themselves with the orders of this earth plane and the various locations.

How these principalities intertwine and operate within our lifespan is unknown. Psychologically, they could impose on our decision-making and overall behavior (unless one is Christ-oriented). Then the sins of the forefathers and mothers who had their adherence to the pagan realms and vice versa could also play a role in this. Nevertheless, the realms of the dominions and principalities do have their existence and are part and parcel of this world.

There is no way that we can control any of these dominions on our own. However, Daniel 10 clearly states that St. Michael the archangel can avert these powers when they are standing in the way. Then, of course, Christ, the crucified and risen Christ, has the overall power to come up against all these dominions.

As mentioned previously, there are those who are aware of the strongholds that dominate the airways, buildings, houses, churches, corporations, states, areas, and even nations as well as individuals. Agnes Sanford, healer, lecturer, and wife of an Episcopalian minister, was very much aware of these dominions, especially those that through some miraculous means with the help of her guardian angel she was able to see for herself. She saw one dominion in the heavens that is very much like this earth plane. She said that it was only a dim copy, as the heavenly one was much more perfect and beautiful in every way. Then she could see the principalities that were further away. She could also see the sacred heavens in which God himself and his holy order abide.

St. John described the splendor of it in every way in Revelation 4. Agnes Sanford was also shown that there was a dominion for the animals, and she encountered the many varieties and detected the very stages they were in.*2

Nevertheless, the sacred sages of the Orient, those who have devoted their whole lives to God, and of course, our Christian saints, have always related the fact that there are definitely many dominions in the heavens. Some of these dominions are definitely opposed to the Christian realms and to the other traditional ones and have powers to go against the holy order.

One of the best ways to explain how these principalities work came about not too long ago. Women's Aglow is a born-again group that exists worldwide. They keep in touch on the Internet and have their conferences and meetings in various places here in the United States, in Europe, and in other countries as well. They posted an emergency prayer alert some time ago in reference to the fact that a principality of the Persian order, Prince of Persia (Daniel 10), had infiltrated the hemisphere of the United States. This in itself revealed that there was a Muslim nation planning to take over on a grand scale.

Soon thereafter, it was announced through the news media that Arabia (Emeric) was planning to control several of the US harbors. The Women's Aglow had already begun their prayer vigils months prior to this announcement; consequently, these plans of the Arabian takeover were quickly eliminated. After all the facts were brought to the fore, the government, being strongly opposed, rapidly took the proper actions in this regard, and all plans were negated.

It is difficult for some to evaluate that all of these realms actually do exist. However, according to those who have had visions and have been assured that there is an afterlife, much more will be disclosed. Then later, when we learn more about outer space, science will disclose further information. But most of all, the important factor is in regard to the fact that there is always the overpowering presence of the dominions of the Trinity—Father, Son, and Holy Ghost—that always still makes its presence known. Even though the huge faring contractors do try to block and eliminate the holy order in whatever way they can, the power, light, and presence of the sacred order supersedes all, even all that is part and parcel of this earth and its varied and multiple controls over and in this universe as well as the realms of the ancestral domains that clutch and leach around individuals.

The fact that this very holy composite is there and that we can have access to it gives an individual the realization that one is truly fortunate and blessed to be a part of the Christian heritage in every way. All dominions and powers are subject to Christ. It states in the Bible, "For in Him dwelleth all the fulness of the Godhead bodily. And ye are complete in Him which is the head of all principality and power."(Col 2:9&10) Every power in this universe is subject to Him.

The angels of the churches and the Trinity certainly stand before God, and they work and continue to do so to the unity of mankind according to God's power and will. However, there are dominions that control and reign in another realm and work to oppose this matter of the holy order in whatever manner they can. This sets up the combustion of star wars—good against evil. Sometimes these dominions are steeped in mere stupidity and the realms of sheer ignorance, leading astray that which God hopes to restore and redeem.

All of this aurora borealis is constantly at work in our midst on many different levels. There is only one way to keep things stable in one's life and circumstances, and that is through Christ. This was the reason of His passion; any other avenue or path goes merely into the debris of paganism and leads away from the holy order.

The power and light of the Trinity is ever present in the Holy Eucharist and certain locations on earth in the churches in which the holy order within the blessed sacrament is established and where His presence is sustained. As Christians, we have access to it, and we can place dominions and their legions within that scope and ask for the necessary help whenever needed. Areas and places of work and residences can be placed within the holy order whenever needed.

Star wars are certainly a part of this universe on all different levels, and when we are aware of their combustion, they add an exciting phenomena to the realms of our daily lives. Some can even see the color flashes around us that can stagger the imagination. Walter Wink phrases it quite clearly in his book in which he explains the many aspects of these many realms that are at work all around us at all times. At one point, he states,

> War in heaven—every event on earth has its heavenly counterpart. Thus when David was about to attack the Philistines, Yahweh counseled attack from the rear: And when you hear the sound of marching (the angelic army) in the tops of the balsam trees, then bestir yourself; for then the Lord has gone out before you to smite the army of the Philistines (2 Sam. 5:24).

GOD'S PURPOSE

--------•●✿●•--------

G od's purpose is to bring us ever closer to
His will. That is a tall order in itself. Then
what is His will to begin with? It is clearly
defined in some, especially those who are aiming to
lead religious lives. But His will is essentially the same
within everyone, and that is to bring us closer to Him
and His everlasting love.

Our priorities in this fast lifestyle are certainly
diversified, and the demands made upon us in the workaday
world can and do enmesh our thinking and behavior into
a collective materialistic type of business mode. We have
to accommodate co-workers and collaborate with the
higher brass in so many ways. The requirements are to
make the money that sustains the lives of our families and
ourselves. There is no way in which we can escape this.

Many are tuned in primarily to the ways and
mentality of society, the media, and the demands of

others and the ways of this world. But then, God's purpose for everyone is quite different. Some are to serve mankind in the field of science or medicine—to bring the cures and healing that are required. Others contribute their time and energies to other causes that also enhance the human dilemma on this earth in a variety of ways.

Nevertheless, everyone, I think, has an inner radio or inner tuning to God's work or intention for us. In our quieter moments, we can get a glimpse of this, and we can see or begin to see where our lives are leading. This is, of course, the time when we take inventory to see if it is going along the way God had intended it to go or whether we are being led astray on a path that is leading away from the intended purpose.

Sometimes an individual is led along into an extremely problematic situation or placed within grievous circumstances in order to evaluate what the primary goal is to be. Agnes Sanford, well-known healer and writer, went through a period in which she suffered from extreme depressions; it was so bad that she continuously sought help from physicians and healers in order to alleviate its intense stronghold. It was during this time that she suddenly realized and remembered that there had been a confrontation with Christ long ago when she was not yet on this earth.

She remembered that Christ had spoken to her and explained to her what her task in this life was to be and that she had to overcome certain things within herself in order to fulfill the requirements of becoming a healer. She found a healer who cured her instantaneously and lifted the depressions from her. Then she proceeded to do the job that Christ had assigned her to do.★1

Some have holy experiences in this life, and God or Christ appears in order to instruct us to do a certain thing at a certain time. Catherine Marshall had the incredibly beautiful experience to see Christ when she was very ill with a severe lung infection. She had been told by her physician that there would be no hope for her and that her disease had become fatal. She went to her parents' home in order to die. It was then, one night, that Christ appeared to her and told her that she would be healed completely and that she could then continue to do the work God had in store for her.

Her parents took her back to the doctor the following day, and after the usual x-rays and tests were taken, it was shown that she was completely healed of the disease. What a celebration that was for the whole family. She wrote several books thereafter in order to tell the world of the wonderful works of God and the immense power and love God has in store for us.★2

I myself had an intense and unexpected confrontation with the holy order when I was still very young. In the Far East, some illnesses can be severe, and during those years, a life can be taken quickly. At that time, there were no antibiotics as yet. I had blood poisoning in my leg, and I knew that as little as I was, I had little or no strength in my whole body and was not able to walk at that time. The illness kept getting worse, and the fever drained much of my vitality each day. Then one night, one of God's elders appeared to me.

Even though I had had little or no religious education at that time, I knew this saint well. He was tall and graceful. His face was framed with a beautiful white beard and long white hair. He was surrounded by a strong light and wearing a long white robe. He lifted me out of bed and comforted me. I told Him that there was just no hope. He quickly told me that if I wanted to come home, I could do so but then reminded me that I had come upon this earth for a specific reason.

My mother had lost five children, and I had been sent to alleviate this dreadful sorrow. I could come home; however, I was then shown what the consequences would be on my family. Much more was explained, plus further reasons for this life that I cannot go into.

Nevertheless, since I had been given the choice and could see the sorrow that would be bestowed on the family, I quickly decided that I had to stay in order to fulfill God's plan for me even though the road ahead would be a difficult one. It did not take long before I became well once again and was enriched with the knowledge that God does have a definite purpose for everyone.

Corrie Ten Boom, while waiting for a bus in the Netherlands, summed it up in so many ways. She had not too long ago come out of the horrid concentration camp Ravensbruck and was standing there on the street where she had stood some years ago when she was younger and prior to the war. She thought back on those earlier years. Here she was, completely dressed up in a new dress, new shoes, and a new purse. All of this apparel would have meant so much to her prior to the war, and even though she was grateful for them, her priorities had changed drastically.

She knew that there was nothing on this earth that would take the place of God's daily direction in her life. During the heavy years in Ravensbruck and its fierce and detrimental hours, God had taught her that there was nothing and no one who could be her refuge except Christ Himself. She realized the immensity of her riches then and continued to lecture and write about His holy order for some years until it was time for her to return home. ★3

How can something be God's purpose when we have to go through concentration camps, live with chronic illnesses that leave us on the sidelines, accept sudden and premature deaths of parents or children, lose jobs, or have to live in sheer poverty due to circumstances? The deluge and sorrows can overtake our lives to such an extent that one's faith in God is not only diminished, but can also be obliterated completely. The million-dollar question is this: "How can God allow this to happen?"

In Deuteronomy, the passage of the Ten Commandments is clear. However, I have noticed that in some Bibles, the full text does not appear. God spoke to Moses face-to-face and described and gave the laws that are part and parcel of our existence. In the passage in which God gives the instructions concerning our dedication and homage to God, He says,

> Thou shalt have no other Gods before me. Thou shalt not make any graven image (idolatry). Thou shalt not bow down thyself unto them, nor serve them: for I the

Lord thy God am a jealous God, visiting the iniquity of the fathers upon the children unto the third and fourth generation of them that hate me. (Deut 5:9)

This is the gist of God's anger. The holocaust can be a continuous one throughout the generations if not adhered to. I know that within my own ancestry, the sins of the forefathers and mothers were horrid crimes. I could see the deluge of this upon the present generation of our own family. My own parents' families in the past were jewels when it came to their dedication and homage to Christ. However, these other matters of extreme heresies in the branches within one's family can only be eradicated by bringing them into the Holy Eucharist and doing this repeatedly. Ask God to forgive the sins of the forefathers and mothers who prayed and collaborated with false gods.

The computer is an incredibly wonderful invention, and I have been familiar with several software programs. In one of them, Word Perfect, which is not used much now, there is a particular feature whereby you can go into the basic format in reference to the composition you have typed out. In this format, you can see the original commands you have put in reference to the article you are working on. These are in relation to the indentations, paragraphs, style of lettering, and other elements. None of these can be changed unless you go into this particular feature; these are then the commands behind the scenes, so to speak.

So it is in relation to our own lives. Unless we know what the lives were like in the family ancestry, it is difficult to ascertain the results of our own. We are the product of these generational habits and behaviors, genetically and otherwise.

Even though we are not certain of the various sins in our bloodlines, we can list the major ones and bring this to the altar during the Holy Communion. We can list the ones that we do know about and then list the general sins, such as murder, theft, abortions, occult involvement, etc. Whatever the ancestry might have been a part of, we can put this on a list. It has been revealed in the United Kingdom that occult practices in the past ancestry, sometimes generations long ago, bring about mental illness. If and when we continue brining this to the Eucharist, much healing and restoration in the present families can occur.

However, God can and does impose a cross on us in many instances, whether we had bad ancestry or not. I was in an art workshop recently in which we were to create a painting in reference to an important Scripture in the Bible. It was close to Easter, and one of the young women had completed her work in just about one hour. She then said quite triumphantly that she was quite satisfied with the painting and was not going to change it in any way.

As I looked at it, I saw a huge cross in the middle of the page, taking up most of the room. On one side, there was rocky terrain, and on the other side, behind it, there was a blue sky with some clouds. She explained that it was really all very simple. The rocky terrain was the earth, and we could not get to heaven on the other side without going through that large cross. We had to pass in and through it completely before we were allowed to go into heaven. This was certainly a single-minded and clear way to demonstrate the way of the cross.

Sometimes a cross imposed on our lives can be one of a greater magnitude than we had bargained for. The advice in the Bible is subtle. St. Paul said, "In everything give thanks;
for this is the will of God in Christ concerning you." (Thess. 5:18) In Habakkuk, there is further explanation: "Although the fig tree shall not blossom, neither shall fruit be in the vines; the labor of the olive shall fail, and the fields shall yield no meat; the flock shall be cut off from the fold, and there shall be no herd in the stalls: Yet will I rejoice in the Lord, I will joy in the God of my salvation." (Hab. 3:17&18) This is a sure way to keep in a positive and good frame of mind when confronted with the cross.

It is not easy to rejoice when your inner self is broken from the weight and grief of hardship. There is only one place where this grief can be turned around, and this is in and through the Holy Eucharist. The Holy Communion is the closest union to Christ. To ask for inner healing for the pain and hardship can be an everlasting revelation. The light and healing power of Christ are the strongest there is. This is His passion, and it shoots through the rocky road and dense and devious realms of an almost unbelieving spirit, and the soul within can receive this instantaneously!

His passion reaches much further than this, for this was God's purpose. His holy order tries to touch our lives here on this earth, sometimes through detriment, heartache, and suffering. God finally reaches us, and Christ takes over so that we do not remain in the stagnant clutches of the pagan realms. This earth, its development, its great inventions, and accomplishments of science, art, and medicine are all part of God's intervention. However, our inner places and where we are aiming for in the hereafter leaves us walking a tightrope, as these are indeed on a level of the unknown.

Therefore, it is God's purpose to lead us into His heavenly place and not to let us become engrossed and swept up into the collective consciousness of this world—the continuous aim for material gain, so to speak. We must remain conscious of His love and direction and the repeated effort to link ourselves to the stronghold of the holy order. This can be obtained by weekly church attendance and also our own prayer lives, which we should seek faithfully on a daily basis.

It is in and through these means that we can learn God's purpose and will for our lives and families. And through this continuous effort, it can be revealed to us what His purpose is actually all about—a revelation that can be astounding in more ways than one if we persist in our efforts.

RETREAT

————•●✸●•————

There are many who have never gone on a retreat or thought of taking the time off to do so. However, it is the most precious time of one's life when it can be done. The time set aside is an extremely special and holy time, for it is devoted to hours and minutes spent totally in God's presence. Retreat offers a time to pray, meditate, and reflect on one's life. At other times, it helps to solve a particular problem. Sometimes the weight and sorrow of a problem can be so devastating and enormous that the mind is clouded with confusion, bewilderment, anger, or grief. This in itself can be released and helped through a retreat, and the inner pain or difficulties involved can be dealt with rationally and spiritually.

A retreat is always beneficial, and after one emerges from the time spent in quietude, meditation, and reflection, an individual can feel refreshed, no matter whether the problem has been solved or not. An answer will be on the horizon in the near future, and the restoration of mind, soul, and spirit can be felt quite innately.

Life seems to envelop individuals in such a way that specific modes of the establishment begin to play an overly important role in their lives. Involvement with friends and acquaintances and pressures and demands of one's job are decidedly directed by the influence of society's requirements. One is almost commanded to run with the pack, so to speak, at times.

Each generation brings new ideas and standards of its own, and these are again changed when the next generation comes to the fore. The bluing of America becomes the greening, purpling, or graying—whatever the influence of the sociological scheme dictates at the time. The enmeshments of these codes and demands begin to regulate one's thinking and behavior.

The media is a large contributor of this through the news and television. We can see, for instance, that within a series of TV shows or skits that are viewed weekly, certain methods of conduct and mentalities are standard among whatever group one associates with. These travailing actions and thought patterns become almost like a conditioned reflex after a while.

When we draw away from them and think that in actuality, our lifespans are merely specks in reference to the billions of years this earth has existed, the realization comes to the fore that what we usually pursue on the whole becomes rather trivial. The earth has existed for 18 billion years, give or takes 1.1 billion; our little yearly lifespans are only drops in the bucket of the overall scheme of things.

Where will we be billions of years from now? What will be, and where will we be in the remaining billions of years when we get out of this fleeting lifespan? It is important to prepare ourselves spiritually for that future journey when we leave this earth. When you really begin to think about it more deeply, emphasis on the mundane matters of this life becomes almost irrelevant.

Perhaps circumstances have turned in such a way so that out of necessity, one has to find a specific answer to one's problems. Life's events and participating pressures become the criteria by which an individual actually can remove himself or herself from any kind of spiritual involvement. One is often looked upon or labeled a fanatic if he or she does not run along with society's set of rules; it can set one apart from the so-called norm, be frowned upon, or make one the odd man out.

Participation in church is already an accomplishment, and we begin to ask questions that had not occurred to us before. But then a change can take place—a turn of events where more direct answers are needed on special needs, events, or occurrences. A time to find the direction and help of the holy order cannot be eradicated. Sometimes this can lead to deeper, better spiritual lives within ourselves—and more demand on our parts to pray and be directed can be indicated.

This keener sense of awareness of these needs can be a new steppingstone to a better life and a more spiritual direction on the whole. The result is a deeper and intense way in prayer when we mature in our spiritual lives and seek God's inner voice.

You might say of a retreat, "Well, this costs money; I cannot spend this extra cash right now" or "How can I possibly spend any extra time? My job demands full hours, and so does my family, and other social activities require that I am there and cannot be missed." However, when we really are serious about wanting inner direction and a closer walk with God and Christ, we can make the time, even when we are too busy. This time can be set aside in our own homes, and a simple retreat can be organized for a day such as Saturday or another day when you are not at work. You can view the weeks ahead and pick a day during which you can steer away from family, friends, work, and responsibilities.

You have to be serious and definite about this arrangement, for moments spend with God are precious. Then you can plan the whole day ahead. Either take the phone off the hook or put it in another location. Tell the family about it, and ask not to be disturbed. Be sure not to be sidetracked by television, neighbors, or other well-meaning family members or friends. When there is a pressing problem, this is the best way to tackle the immediate circumstances in relation to it.

The Bible relates that some problems can only be solved by fasting and prayer, and this is exactly the direction to take, as the day is totally dedicated to prayer and fasting. Pick a particular day, and then setting everything else aside, proceed with the following. Early in the morning, you can start with either tea or coffee and juice but no solid food. Then devote yourself to an hour of prayer. Use a prayer book and/or various prayers and litanies that you have used previously.

Read in the Bible for a while, and go into contemplative prayer and inner direction after the prayers. Bring your special problem to the fore. Ask God's guidance and constructive advice in regard to the petition at hand. Have a notebook handy, and record anything special that is given inwardly or any thoughts that are helpful in any way. Drink plenty of water during these hours.

At lunchtime, take a glass of juice, tea, or water and some protein powder mixed with it in order to keep you from thinking too much about food. Whatever comes to mind to keep you in the meditative mood should be followed. Directly before or after lunch, again devote another time for prayer and listening within. It is helpful to ask your priest or minister to pray for you—especially for this retreat day—to give you inner quietude and direction.

When we are not accustomed to finding an inner quietude for an extended period, there are many emotions and feelings that at first will begin to emerge. They can be depression, headaches, hunger, and intense boredom. Monica Furlong describes some of the beginnings of these attempts. "Of course to begin with, silence is not silence at all; it is filled with our own perpetual inner chatter. As this gradually dies away, we begin to feel we know the silence intimately, almost like a person."[*1] She explains that extreme boredom is a smokescreen for fear—a fear that can come upon the horizon, fear of the unknown, fear of death, fear of isolation, etc. It is then the aim to move beyond the so-called inner chatter and inner pain and come to know the inner silence in which and through which we find God in contemplation and constant inner prayer.

The inner conflict can become extremely intense, for it is at this point where we surrender, and this is precisely the criteria we are looking to achieve—a surrender to the silence and the direction and will of God.

This practice of going into a retreat is not an easy one, as our society as a whole is so focused on outer stimulation—anything and everything to keep busy—noise, music, radio, and TV to blot out our very thoughts. Continuity is then the essential part of prayer. We must move into stillness and inner peace. Then we must determine to achieve the intended results.

In the afternoon, a walk in the garden could be taken, or a rest time could be set aside. But do not turn on the radio or television. Also, to keep the hunger away, drink plenty of water again in between. This is an excellent way to clear the intestinal tract as well. Late in the afternoon, have another prayer time for further direction, read the Bible, or say various litanies if you feel so inclined. Again, listen for inner direction coming forth. Sometimes direction is not given during the day of the retreat but several days thereafter.

End the retreat before dinner time, which you can take early. Finish reading some Scripture, and thank God for whatever you are thankful for. Ask to be given further direction as time progresses. Then at dinnertime, break the fast, and take a light supper. This is a marvelous way to have a closer walk with God and Christ. Also put the notebook aside for the next time to be used during the retreat, and see what has been accomplished in the meantime during the week or weeks that followed the last retreat.

Of course, there are retreats that can be taken through the church and with a group instead of on your own. Some are guided retreats, and others are silent retreats. They can last from one to three days or perhaps a week. They are usually excellent and can be taken in accordance with what your needs are.

You can also partake in a mini retreat that lasts for a period of seven days but allows you to proceed with a regular work schedule. This is done in the following manner. The Franciscan friars have a fine booklet on this. Start each day with reading some Psalms and a Daily Mission Prayer for a private retreat.

> Lord, my God, I dedicate this week of retreat to the honor of the most Holy Trinity. Please come to my assistance, and help all those who are making this spiritual exercise. Filled with sorrow, as I am, for my past failures to love you and my neighbor, I am grateful beyond measure for all the graces and favors you have given me in the years gone by. Now, in your goodness and mercy, help me to live each day of this retreat in your company so I will learn better how to do your work in the world to the best of my ability. These favors I ask through the merits of Christ, our Savior, as I rely on the aid of the ever-blessed Virgin Mary, the holy angels, and all the saints. Amen.

When you have finished this prayer, say an invocation prayer, such as, "Come to my assistance, O God; Lord, make haste to help me." Continue with a Scripture reading, and then say a Litany and perhaps some other prayers and your request.

Then proceed with your regular schedule for the day, whether it is housework, your job, or some other occupation. Try each hour of the day to find a few moments of quiet prayer. A petition prayer such as said above is good, or the Jesus prayer is a fine one so say. "Lord Jesus Christ, Son of God, have mercy upon us."

State again your request, and keep silent for a few seconds. Words are not important; it is a matter of moving into inner stillness and finding inner direction that comes from God. If every hour is too much to cope with in your schedule, try for every two hours or a couple of times a day. At least you are keeping in touch with the retreat in this way.

It is important during this week not to dwell too much on any immediate problem or harbor any negative feelings. Whatever your requests are, keep positive in your mental attitude, no matter how difficult your situation might be. A quote from the booklet says, "Everyone has moments when nothing goes well, when everything seems to go wrong. Such times test the reality of our confidence in God's goodness, and His constant care of us. You must then make a particular effort to learn how to lean on God alone when the going is hard."*2

In the evening, before bedtime, return once more to the moments of the retreat. Go over your own regular prayers, and spend time listening within. Close with the following retreat prayer.

I thank you, Father in heaven, for all the inspirations and blessings of this mission. I implore your continuing assistance in the days ahead. With your unfailing help, I firmly hope to know your will for me and to do it faithfully in all the events of my life.

Please send your Holy Spirit to aid me to be another Christ to everyone I encounter and to have His mind in all I plan or do.

Now that I cast all my cares upon you, loving Father, I am confident that you will be my protector in every necessity. I trust that you will fulfill all my requests, as you have promised us.

I adore you, God almighty, Father, Son, and Holy Spirit, and by your power, I rededicate myself and all who are dear to me to your service. Amen.

Continue each day to do the same and keep up this special mini retreat for seven days. If you can, also keep a dairy of special directions you are receiving during this time, and then again go over all of these when you reach the end of the seven days.

Another kind of retreat consists of a half-day retreat that can also be very beneficial. This is especially good when you have a difficult schedule and still would like to have this time of quiet prayer. During the morning hours, some time can be set aside. This can be done when you first wake up, or for instance, from 8:00 a.m. until noontime. It is important to fast and just take in plenty of water until it is lunchtime. You can start with the initial prayers and/or litanies, thereafter making the special requests, and then dedicate the rest of the hours to listening inwardly. Finish with special prayers at about noon. This small retreat can be extremely helpful, and a light lunch to top it all off makes it all the better.

It is vital during any retreat to learn to lean on God alone and listen to guidance. As a consequence, the retreat—whichever one is taken—can be a most instructive, innovative, and incredible learning experience besides the spiritual growth and guidance received during this period.

PRAYER

·•◎•·

While I was driving out in the country to visit a friend one day, I took a wrong turn. It was a half hour and many miles later before I realized that I was on the wrong road. Nothing looked familiar to me, and suddenly, I was at the end of a dead-end street. I was quite annoyed with myself, realizing that I had gone all that distance, and even though I had not recognized certain unfamiliar landmarks, I still continued on that same road.

When I began to think about it, I was aware of the fact that this is what can happen in one's life as well; the wrong road can be taken. However, this wrong turn can be rectified, even though the mileage might have been lengthy. Having traveled roads that we have organized in a specific way and then realizing that this is not working out as was planned can be a dead end in more ways than one. But then perhaps it was not destined to be, and we simply have to direct ourselves in a different direction.

Sometimes illnesses, a loss of a job, death, or a failed marriage can be the factors, and we are then confronted with life-altering situations. It is then that we have to turn deeply inward and find the method to deal with our dilemmas and lives on a different level and use willpower and common sense in order to change things. But most of all, one can rely upon the old, sacred habit of prayer.

Prayer is your lifeline to God and Christ. It is your stronghold; when you pray, you are calling upon God's holy order (Trinity) and seeking His contact, help, and intervention.

However, it is difficult to pray to God when you have lost the connection, so to speak, or when you have never been certain of His holy realm. We can become lost and disoriented when we are confronted with grief or any dilemma, and it is necessary to know that there truly is a holy order of God and Christ to help and bail you out. Sometimes one is fortunate, and after having sought help, the difficulties are eliminated, but sometimes it takes months and even years to eradicate the problem. But the main objective is to realize that God's holy order does exist, even though we are not aware of it many times.

In order to be fortified in the faith, it is helpful to go to church on a regular basis. When you hear the sermons and take part in the Holy Eucharist, your faith is renewed, and if in the beginning, it is difficult, no matter how much opposition you might come up against, fight in order to get there at least once a week. Confirmation in a church steeped in Christ is preferable, and it is also necessary to continue to seek help from the ministry. If you prefer a female minister, seek a church devoted to Christ that has a female minister. If you are a Catholic, a nun can be a wonderful instrument of God's help.

But above all, "Pray without ceasing" (1 Thessalonians 5:17), as the Bible says. Agnes Sanford, the late healer and author, mentions that before you begin your prayer, always ask for protection from Christ. This in itself is a safeguard. There are many forces, principalities, and dominions around us that are certainly not of the holy order. You cannot fight the invisible enemy unless you devote and unite yourself with God and Christ and Their holy order. We ourselves do not have the resources to do this; only God and Christ can intercede and alter much in our lives.

When life has dealt its severest blows, whether they are illnesses, loss of home, loss of job, friction within the family, a bad marriage, loss of friends—whatever difficulties, trauma will remain. Therefore, it is good to go to a healing service, if possible and find one in your neighborhood. Keep going as much as possible, and during the Eucharist, keep asking God to heal the inner pain and shocks, whether they be mental, spiritual, physical, or within the soul, which is on a deeper level.

In order to sustain ourselves within the protective care and love of God the Father and Christ, it is important to unite ourselves anew with Him each and every day. Set aside some time in the morning for prayer. Get up a half hour earlier, and set that time apart. A good prayer book is also beneficial. I use St. Augustine's *Prayer Book* (Holy Cross Publications, West Park, NY). You can inquire at a good Christian bookstore about other prayer books. You can also use the *Common Book of Prayer* from the Church of England or the Episcopalian Church in the United States. Go over the prayers listed for the morning and evening, and make your choices accordingly.

During this quiet time, it is important to read in the Bible. Bible reading is important, and it is good to do so whenever you can. The church often has a day-by-day pamphlet that can be used daily with a lesson and Scripture in addition to your meditation period. A list can be made up of all the things you consecrate to Abba and Christ; then you can commit certain particular problems and other matters to Him at that time as well. I usually end these sessions by asking for the blessing and unction of the Holy Spirit upon my circumstances, my family, and myself.

If you are so inclined, after you have said the prayers, you can also devote some time to listening within. We are directed to live in the Spirit, and during prayer time, we turn to the inner room. I call this the intercom system between God and Christ and self. St. Ignatius Loyola said, "Our Lord speaks inside the soul without the din of words raising it up wholly to His Divine Love." The joy of God's love is great, and to dwell in it is a revelation in itself. But it takes time to reach that inner peace, and it takes perseverance to keep seeking it at all costs.

For the evening prayer, again, set aside the time—from half an hour to one hour—and go over the things that have taken place during the day. There are always things that we have done that go directly against the holy order. Sometimes these are done because of sheer ignorance, or sometimes because we deliberately invite them upon ourselves either due to peer pressure or just wanting to go along with the crowd. Whatever the reason, ask God to reveal any past mistakes or sins and ask forgiveness. You can use these prayers out of the prayer book. If we can recall that we have transgressed against the will of God in a certain instance, it should be brought to the fore. These wrong actions of the past can sometimes bring about a deluge of sorrows. To go to confession, if possible, is preferable.

Another way to reach a better insight into things is to read a good religious book. This can help to give further spiritual direction, and you can always learn through what others have to teach in their writings. Read some of its text during your meditation time in the evening. Ask God to come into your immediate problems and direct your way so you can find all the necessary solutions. Thank Him for the blessings He has bestowed upon you during the day, and ask for protection and healing during the night.

If and when you feel particularly downcast and depressed, read the old fourteenth-century prayer *Anima Christi:*

> Soul of Christ, sanctify me. Body of Christ, save me.
> Blood of Christ, inebriate me. Water flowing from the

side of Christ, wash me. Passion of Christ, strengthen me. O good Jesus, hear me. Hide me within Thy wounds. Never permit me to be separated from Thee. From the malignant enemy, defend me. And bid me to come to Thee. That with thy saints, I may praise Thee. For everlasting ages.

"Pray without ceasing,"(1Thess.5:17) the Bible says. You can do this wherever you are on a bus, train, or plane or during business hours. When work is a burden and you have too much to cope with, the Jesus prayer is helpful and easy to remember: "Lord Jesus Christ, Son of God, have mercy upon me." You can say this repeatedly.

No matter what affiliation you are from, prayers from another church can be helpful as well—and sometimes better than the ones we have known. Some use the rosary frequently, even though they are not Catholic. President Ronald Reagan requested one of the priests in Medjugorje to present his prayers to the Holy Mary, who had been appearing in these regions for some years. These prayers were in regard to some of his major negotiations in the political arena.

Whether you are a Protestant, Anglican, or Catholic, the Divine Mercy Prayer is a confrontation with God, asking His intervention and mercy. These prayers are extremely powerful and miraculous in every way. They can change circumstances, alter the difficulties in a person's life, or for those for whom we pray, deter any kind of evil and halt an attack from the enemy and therefore protect whenever there is need of this.

In several instances, I have seen a tremendous change in people's lives when they prayed the Divine Mercy Prayers—wonderful and beautiful changes!

Sr. Faustina Kowalska was given this form of prayer by Christ to give it to the world. This prayer is very important and is able to reach within so many different areas, it would fill pages in order to write about its benefits. If it is difficult for an individual to pray, then this would be a beautiful way to reach God and request His mercy and direction. It is a reliable means that will ultimately bring one closer to the holy order. These famous prayers can be ordered from The Divine Mercy, Marian Press, Stockbridge, MA, 01263.

When we hear news concerning the deluge of fighting, wars, famines, and earthquakes taking place in the world today, it is as if a certain anarchy in man and nation is prevalent within the nations. You begin to wonder if God is available in this universe when He allows these types of atrocities to take place. The grief and sorrow are so great in specific places that people are beginning to question how a merciful God can allow these things to happen. But there are certain laws in this universe, and if and when man transgresses these laws, the outcome can be detrimental, and innocent ones are also affected.

In Matthew 24, we read, "There shall be famines, pestilence and earthquakes in diverse places." It further reads, "Ye shall hear of wars and rumors of wars," then again, "All these are the beginning of sorrows." But then, "But he that shall endure unto the end, the same shall be saved." (Math. 24:6 ,7&13)This should be kept in mind at all costs. There is a chance that one may be persecuted when one follows Christ. This is not always the case; however, sometimes it is. But the ultimate test is to endure and keep the faith, no matter if things are falling apart in this world. "But he that shall endure unto the end, the same shall be saved."(Math.24:13)

Nevertheless, in order to ensure our own protection and direction, we should keep praying each and every day and actually try to pray without ceasing whenever we are confronted with any hardships. Unfortunately, in some areas, the degrading actions and mentality of society are already revealing themselves today. The lifestyle and morals are very different from a few years ago. In a society in which there is so much change and new concepts and laws are constantly enforced, renewed, and then changed again, it is important to stay very close to our trust in God with secure and sound prayer lives.

THE HOLY EUCHARIST

———•●❋●•———

L ife can get extremely complicated, and we can be engulfed with the most severe difficulties, such as illnesses, loss of family, loss of employment, or loss of home and goods. Calamities can overshadow our lives or a nation at certain times. Nevertheless, as Christians, we have access to all the help necessary. Problems can be eradicated, or they can be altered—not only through prayer, but also through the Holy Eucharist.

Christ came into this world especially to help the poor. He was born in a stable, but He was omnipresent. He came especially in order to lead an individual to God and His Holy Trinity and to make one realize the importance of this. The duration of our lives is only a drop in a bucket of water, and we have to realize that we will continue in the hereafter for millions of years to come. Where we will be depends a great deal on our actions here on earth during these limited years.

There is much in Christianity we do not yet know or understand, especially when a religion has been dealt with in such a superficial manner in certain circles. It eliminates its very essence and its core of wisdom as well.

Jesus ascended from this earth; however, He left us with a realm of gold and wealth far removed from the material concept this earth has in relation to wealth and gold. He left us, in reality, with His holy presence in the Eucharist. This Holy Communion, with its element of true holiness, is in reality very difficult to contemplate. When we partake of this Eucharist, we become engulfed in His actual presence and its frequency of light, which is extremely powerful.

We have been taught from early on that we come into His holy presence in order to ask forgiveness of our sins. But the sins of our forefathers can also be mentioned and be given at certain times—suicides, occult involvements, miscarriages, murder, curses, abortions, the war dead, fornication, and adultery—all of these can be placed on the altar.

During the Holy Communion, the names and actions (if known) of the ancestry can also be placed into the sacred sacrament—especially when we are dealing with illnesses and tragedies of various kinds in our present lives. "For the Lord thy God am a Jealous God, visiting the iniquity of the fathers upon the children unto the third and fourth generation of them that hate me" (Deuteronomy 5:9). Occult involvement of any kind in our bloodlines can continue to play a detrimental role today in various forms. As a precautionary measure, it is good to place these into the Holy Eucharist as much as is required.

The fact is that Christ's holy presence is so powerful in its frequency and love that we can ask and submit much more into this actual holy union. We do not realize the magnificence of its value, grace, and power. Many, many miracles take place when we give certain problems into Christ's hands in and during the Holy Communion. Bob and Penny Lord, in their book *Miracles of the Eucharist,* said, "The gleam of the sun is like the life giving rays of the Eucharist. It nourishes us. It warms us. It gives us life when it shines on us, we are enveloped in the compassion of His Love."*1

Christ gave the ultimate sacrifice; that in itself enables us to be in His realm of the Holy Trinity (for a short period), which contains the light of the holy order, a frequency so high that the realm of physics has not even ascertained it as yet. We can be more than grateful for this, as it gives us a gift of such magnitude where we can freely place our problems, concerns, and requests each and every time.

As the many miracles have taken place during the centuries, I would like to enumerate on this and relate some true events that have taken place during and after some very special requests given during this holy event by certain individuals.

When my grandson was about two years old, he developed asthma. The child became continuously choked up with this malady, and the nebulizer became a constant companion in his daily routine. His wheezing and coughing were dreadful each and every day, and it was heartbreaking for his parents and I to see this little boy suffer this way. This went on for a couple of years, not getting any better, but it seemed almost worse at times. Then two wonderful missionary friends of mine and I decided to take this hardship to the Holy Eucharist.

These two missionaries had lived in China and the UK. Bruce was a brother of Professor Hiram Bingham from Yale, who had founded Machu Picchu. Bruce and his wife had had a great deal of experience, having taken many with the most severe illnesses through a special and innate form of prayers and always with successful results. This time, we placed the names of the ancestry on the altar and little Jonathan's name alongside of them. We prayed diligently over this very serious form of illness, placing it into the Holy Eucharist, and in a few months, the attacks became less and less. My grandson was cured within a few months. At that time, he was about fourteen years of age. Today, he is twenty-one years of age, in good health, and completing his studies at a university.

A few years ago, my cousins from Canada called to let me know that their first grandchild had been born— such excitement. A beautiful little girl by the name of Alyssa had made her entrance into the world. However, approximately two months later, they came with the unfortunate news that the new baby had been diagnosed with meningitis. It was a severe case, and they had been told that Alyssa would never develop normally and that the future held little promise.

A year followed in which the little infant went through the most horrendous treatments in order to try to cure this disease. She was maintained with a respirator, wires and tubes were placed all over her small body, and she was mostly puffed up due to the retention of fluids within. The little baby also began to have a series of seizures. Then the repeated tests in between and the MRIs in order to evaluate the results caused further complications.

The physicians kept emphasizing that there was little hope for this small infant. Family in Canada, Europe, and the United States prayed around the clock. We have a prayer chain here in the United States, and bringing this immense hardship to the Holy Eucharist was a priority.

But then each month, things began to change slowly at first, and one year later, little Alyssa had regained all her faculties and became a normal, healthy baby, ready and eager to respond to life in every way. Today she is four years old and a beautiful, healthy, normal youngster. She does have a little problem with her speech now and then, but with some therapy and special reading lessons, this will not be a problem at all. The doctors say that her condition and its healing were enormous miracles not expected by the medical arena.

The Holy Communion is beautifully endowed with not only the essence of its immense power, but also with the power of healing. Not too long after having gone through a trying period in my own life and circumstances due to the death of two very close friends, I was deeply depressed and in need of some help.

As I went to church one particular Sunday, I asked God and Christ to heal my inner frustration, grief, and disappointments. I began this prayer in the beginning of the Holy Communion. As I did so, I was suddenly immersed in an overpowering ray of light that went to the most inner part of my whole being and soul. Its warmth and rays fluctuated even around my whole self. It was so overpowering that it caused tears to come to my eyes.

When I walked out of that church after that beautiful Eucharist, I was uplifted and completely overtaken by the immense holy power of God and its healing. My grief and frustrations were left behind and did not return again. I was also touched by an inner knowledge and healing in regard to my difficulties that I had had to face during the last months; therefore, there was a complete release from it all. This was the second time Christ had healed me; the first time was from an illness I spoke about in another chapter.

The late Dr. Kenneth McAll, eminent physician, psychiatrist, and missionary from the UK, had the ability to see the other side and consequently the line of ancestry an individual is endowed with. Several years ago, when I met with him after his lecture tour in Canada, he immediately spoke to me about the five children my mother had lost and that these souls had not been picked up. These children had died, some during delivery and others several days after their birth—a dreadful tragedy for my mother.

When we attended the Holy Communion the following day, we dedicated these children to Christ and gave them names, after which time they departed in peace to go to the place chosen for them by God. Dr.

McAll often spoke about the many aborted babies—that these too should be prayed over during the Holy Eucharist and be given names and placed in the holy order and Eucharist (the Trinity) so that they can continue to their intended destination.

One of Dr. McAll's most famous events was in regard to the Bermuda Triangle and its involvement. The mystery of the ships and planes that suddenly disappeared was a tremendous tragedy, and no one seemed to be able to know what was taking place in these waters. The physician gave a direct explanation in regard to these events when he and his wife, while on a trip to Bermuda, were unexpectedly placed in these waters. The events that followed were totally unforeseen, and in his book, *Healing the Family Tree,* he narrated the whole incident as follows:

> It is not only houses and other buildings that can be freed by this prayer formula. It also works for places which are prone to unusual and otherwise inexplicable accidents such as straight stretches of a particular road or areas of the sky or sea like the much-feared Bermuda Triangle.
>
> For hundreds years the Bermuda Triangle (an area of the Atlantic Ocean enclosed by an imaginary line from Bermuda to Miami to Puerto Rico to Bermuda) had swallowed up ships and aircraft, often without a trace. The sheer weight of the books written on this Subject would sink a small ship. Most sailors prefer to avoid the place but, like many other people, especially landlubbers, I scoffed at such irrational fears. In 1972,

my wife and I were sailing through the "triangle" on a banana boat when we were caught in a force 9 storm. We headed south away from the storm into the infamous Sargasso Sea. There one of the ship's boilers burst, leaving us silently drifting.

In the quietness my wife and I both distinctly heard a strange sound, like a steady droning dirge, which continued throughout the day and night. At first we thought it was the Jamaican crew, but after checking we realized that they were not responsible. Then I found a magazine containing diagrams of the old slave ships, which used this run, with details of how almost two million slaves were thrown overboard. Recently the book Roots by Arthur Hailey was dramatized on television and told movingly of the many dead or dying slaves thrown into the sea on just such a journey. The number of slaves considered unsalable in the West Indies or America increased rapidly as they neared their destination, for conditions on board the slave ships deteriorated even further as the voyage progressed. The merchants often collected more money through insurance for 'lost' slaves than by selling them in Virginia.

When we were back at home in England, it occurred to us that we had heard that mournful dirge for a purpose. Perhaps we had a responsibility to pray for those wretched slaves who died uncommitted to the Lord, and to repent of the cruelty of those who were the cause of it. So, in July 1977, with some interested bishops and some members of the Anglican Community of the Resurrection, a Jubilee Eucharist was celebrated at various places throughout England for the specific release of all those who had met their untimely deaths in the Bermuda Triangle itself, the Anglican Bishop Anselm Ganders and the Reverent Donald Omand, an Anglican priest from Devon, offered the same prayers. The curse of the dreaded place was lifted. From the time of the Jubilee Eucharist until now—five years no known, inexplicable accidents have occurred in the Bermuda Triangle.*2

I heard from Rev. Lloyd Williams (who had worked with Dr. McAll from the late 1980s on) from the UK on May 29, 2009 that there have been no further incidents in those particular regions of the Bermuda Triangle and that the Holy Communions held in England in 1977 were surely instrumental in lifting the detriment causing the tragic accidents. (p114 letter from Rev. Williams Church of England)

Sometimes one Eucharist is sufficient to eradicate a specific problem, but sometimes it is necessary to have a series of them so that the difficulty can be eliminated. Then at other times, because the problems are of long duration or a certain nature, then there is a need of a deeper and stronger prayer request during the Holy Communion. Several churches can collaborate and hold these Eucharists at the same time.

Times are changing, and the Christian church will be persecuted more as time goes on as the Antichrist will be coming to the fore. All of this was predicted in the Bible. Therefore, our stronghold will definitely be more focused on Christ and the Eucharist in the future.

As time goes on, many will push the church and religion further into the background, and society will begin to rely more and more on it own concepts in regard to people's lives and circumstances (also the New Age movement), and the pagan principalities will become more powerful. These dominions and principalities (Ephesians 6) will be powerful and will provoke unrest and discord as time goes on.

It is therefore important to know that all dominions and principalities are subject to Christ. "By the Resurrection of Jesus Christ: Who is gone into heaven, and is on the right hand of God; angels and authorities and powers being made subject unto Him" (1 Peter 3:21–22). As things become more complicated, principalities and dominions can be put into the Holy Eucharist as well as the certain groups or those causing the detriment.

Christ will come again, but we do not know when. Meanwhile, the world and its societies will go along seeking new ways and avenues that will accommodate man's own desires instead of those of the holy church. The Holy Communion is more than a protective measure, and it can alleviate and help in all circumstances, no matter how devious the circumstances are.

One should concentrate on making this world a better place for our children and future generations, realizing that our lifespans are short in comparison to the billions of years this earth has existed and the billions and more that will continue for generations to come. One's life is just a fraction in the totality of eternity. Much is at stake in this short period of time, and the Holy Eucharist gives us an opportunity to link up to the holy order (Trinity) through Christ in order to help us in this life and the next to come.

Our trust is therefore in the Lord. "For I have learned in whatever state I am, therewith to be content" (Philippians 4:11). With the help of Christ, we can be directed and led into contentment as time goes on and realize that our treasures are not in the material, so to speak, but in the trust and peacefulness of the Lord. "Lay not up for yourselves treasures upon earth, where moth and rust doth corrupt and where thieves break through and steal. But lay up for yourselves treasures in heaven, where neither moth nor rust doth corrupt, and steal" (Matthew 6:19–20).

THE LIGHT

And God said, "Let there be Light,"
and there was Light.
—Genesis 1:3

God is Light, and there is no darkness at all in Him.
—John 1:5

God is light, and this light emanates all through the universe and is part of every man. In Revelation 4, there is a complete and wonderful description and explanation of God's holy throne and its light.

There in heaven was a throne with someone sitting on it. His face gleamed like such precious stones as jasper and carnelian and all around the throne was a rainbow the color of emerald. In a circle around the throne were twenty-four other thrones on which were seated 24 elders dressed in white and wearing crowns of gold.

St. John had this beautiful vision while he was still on earth.

Then Moses, during his confrontation with God, had his vision of Him when he was given the Ten Commandments. After he came down from Mount Sinai, where he had been communicating with God, his face also gleamed from God's light, which appeared and was given forth from the fire. The disobedience and unbelief of the people were the dreadful obstructions Moses had to deal with concerning the people. But God's glow and light were revealed on his face as he spoke to the people. This in itself was part of that revelation.

The light sustains the universe, and it is the very being of our existence. Some have the ability to see this light, and some can see the emerald light clearly around some individuals. Sometimes there is a blue light shown, especially during a healing service. Agnes Sanford often saw the blue light being emitted in her many healings she conducted while she was still on this earth.[★1]

The Virgin Mary, whenever her vision has been sighted, also emanates a beautiful blue light and has been seen by a multitude at Fatima, Lourdes, and Garabandal. Our Lady of Medjugorje, who was appearing in Croatia, also emits a holy light and has stated that "We go to Heaven in full conscience and that man receives a transfigured body."[★2] All of the transformations at the time of death are undoubtedly within and through the holy light of God.

Eleonore Prins

Vicka and Jakov, the two visionaries who often saw our lady, had a surprising event with our lady. One afternoon, she took the children to heaven for about twenty minutes. She had told them beforehand that she was going to take them on a journey, and they were looking forward to it. Our Lady of Medjugorje took them to the upper realms, where they had a complete view of heaven. They said that heaven was one huge, endless space. They mentioned specifically that there was a special kind of light there that does not exist on earth. People were dressed in lovely colored clothes, and they were walking, praying, and singing. The children were also aware of a great joy when they were among these people. ★3

St. Paul, who had been persecuting Christians and also took part in the death of St. Stephen, had an incredible confrontation with the light. (Acts 9;:3.4 & 5) gives an account of his experience on the road to Damascus. "As Paul was coming near the city of Damascus, suddenly a light from the sky flashed around him. He fell to the ground and heard a voice saying to him 'Saul, Saul! Why do you persecute me?' 'Who are you, Lord?' He asked. 'I am Jesus, whom you persecute.'"

He was told that he should go to the city, and he would be directed further. As Paul scrambled to his feet, he became aware of the fact that he was blind, and his friends had to help him. They were led into Damascus. For three days, Saul was blind and not able to function. Then Jesus sent a man by the name of Ananias to him in order to heal his affliction. He also filled him with baptism and the Holy Spirit. As Jesus further instructed him, he also told him that he had to suffer later on and after his conversion was complete; he went straight to the synagogues in order to preach about Jesus and His holy order.

God's light is an immensely powerful healing agent. Some years ago, I had an experience with that holy light. I had been ill with septicemia for about one year. The illness had left me extremely weak and despondent as well. My mother had died after a long illness, and this in itself was a devastating memory. Then the sickness had drained me in so many ways that even though all the proper medications had been used, the illness would not leave me. Consequently, I had become quite weary and was almost certain that I would never be well again. Nevertheless, a friend of mine who was considerate and kind had driven me to New York City in order to take part in a healing Mass being conducted by a well-known healer.

As I entered that church, I was convinced that nothing would be able to touch the devastating condition I was in. When I went up to the altar, the priest touched me gently, spoke a few words, and then went to the next individual. I slowly walked back to my seat, and then suddenly, to my complete astonishment as I was still in the aisle, I was completely encircled with the light of God's holy order.

The light was so incredibly strong and heavy that I was not able to keep on standing and consequently fell on the floor. I became aware of the strong sacred odor of Jesus' presence with this light. I knew that I was not able to stand up and waited quietly until I had regained some strength. But then as I was on the floor, I heard a rushing sound, and another light came from behind and immersed the most inner part of my being. I had been certain that nothing could be done, and God was merciful and wonderful to heal even the grief and despondency that I had had for so long.

My whole being was healed—the septicemia and my depressions. It was such a completely holy and beautiful experience to have been in the presence of that holy order and the light that it left me with the conviction that my mother undoubtedly was well cared for on the other side and that I had no cause for worry about her—or myself, for that matter.

In the realm of physics, the light of Jesus and also the light of the holy Mary intercedes and heals infirmities and has all kinds of ramifications within our lives and human network. This light comes from a higher frequency than the lights one encounters here on earth.

Another interesting facet of God's light is that it also emanates on a different frequency as well and is actually part and parcel of the growth, not only of mankind and animals, but also plants. Physicists have discovered that when they took photographs of the light around certain plants in their growing stages, each plant receives the actual color it will display when it matures. The purple eggplant receives an abundant extra purple ray, the tomatoes obtain a red ray, and the blue ray is given to the blue flowers. It operates in the framework differently with each variety. They all are saturated according to the color each one is in need of.

God is forever busily creating new people, animals, and plants in this world and in the outer world as well in our stellar formations. Jim Mullaney, the astronomer, states that when they look into the telescopes each and every day, there are new star formations and entirely new creations to be found. This is on such a magnificent level that he says it is like looking into God's face anew each and every day. Creation is not completed, and He continues to create continuously out in the further expansions of this universe. The spaces between the planets are forever expanding every second and continue to do so every year. The light sustains every part of this universe and its stellar system.

The astronauts on *Apollo 12* who returned from their flight into outer space have commented that they have been strongly aware of God's holy presence while in the air. They have said that this has been especially strong each time they ventured out in their flights.

An interesting phenomena occurred when they landed on the moon the second time. Pictures were taken while these men were walking around the planet, and in these photographs, it showed that each one of them was completely surrounded by a pale blue light: it seemed like a halo surrounded their bodies. NASA did not know what to make of it, so they were never released to the media because of that reason.

Scientists have already come to the conclusion that solar systems like ours can exist. They are presently working on a new planet finder, TPF-C and TPF-1. These spaceships are designed to study the feeble light of any earthlike planets within a forty-five-light year range. They will undoubtedly have to go to the further outer limits of this universe to get any new information. This will not be easy to tackle, as it will be so far away. However, Robert Zimmerman in the magazine *Astronomy 2004* quotes the astronomers who say, "Any day now, any day!" Each and every day, there are more new findings as they probe the skies with their telescopes deeper and further away into the vast span of the universe.

The Lord is the one who made night into day and day into night (Amos 5:8). God sustains all, and to many who are dominated almost entirely by the strongholds and opinions of this world alone, it would be good to stop and think that this earth is approximately 4.5 billion years old. The universe is approximately about 14 billion years old, and our lifespans are merely drops in a bucket—incredibly few years in comparison to the vast span of years of the existence of the world. Some hold fast to what is to be obtained here as they proceed and concentrate merely on its materialistic aspects and negating the spiritual values of this life. There is much waste in the spectrum of this precious lifespan.

The collective consciousness of the corporate world drives a country, the media rides on it, and the pagan dominions run and dictate most of this behind the scenes. These are set to negate and discard the spiritual realms that are innately part of man or woman. It is interesting how these principalities and dominions intertwine and control the world as it is. At times, it seems that they dominate exclusively the whole of things, although God and His Trinity still reign and supersede it all eventually.

If this world had concentrated on the spiritual realms first, how much further would we have progressed along the scientific and medical circuits at this time? Perhaps we would have found a cure for all the ills that assail us if we obeyed the laws of God and His Trinity before all else.

Many cures have been obtained through the Holy light of God and Christ. When one receives the Holy Spirit again, which is called the born-again experience, one receives the realm of light that comes from God directly. This light is a warm ray and enmeshes and engulfs the individual totally into the warm light of the Holy Spirit. This light is extremely powerful. Sometimes one can fall on the ground because of its energy force. Nevertheless, that holy light heals, guides, and directs on all levels. This particular light returns when one is in a healing session, during certain requested prayers in a prayer group, or simply during one's own prayer time when God's guidance has been especially requested. Then especially during the Holy Eucharist, this light comes to the fore again. It is a verification of God's holy presence through the Holy Spirit.

The Christ light from the Trinity can also make its presence known to certain individuals. This light is given at various times after the light of the Holy Spirit has been given previously. In the divine mercy prayer, the famous prayers given to Sister Faustine H. Kowalska from Poland concerning special divine intervention in certain matters, there shown on Christ's picture that there are two lights that are being transmitted. One is a red light, and the other is a white light. The red light would be connected with the Holy Spirit, and the other is on a much higher frequency. Some individuals have the capacity to see these lights when they are in action—a beautiful phenomenon in every way.

Within the New Age categories, there is much speculation concerning the light. In certain parts of Europe, there are spas and institutions that use the light ranges within the electrical arena in order obtain help in the realms of healing. Some of it can be helpful. However, the natural rays from God's throne are on a much higher frequency and reveal themselves on a different plateau.

The New Age movement aligns itself with the pagan dominions and forces, and its territories are on shaky ground. It will leave an individual out on a limb, as its motivation are geared toward the self first instead of helping one's fellow man. There is a concept or belief that it connects with either Hinduism, Buddhism, Shintoism, Taoism, Confucianism, or Islam. However, each one of the Far Eastern religions has its own rules, clings to its own magnetic energy force, and ultimately takes care of its own and is not an outreach of manmade New Age rules. There is a reason why they are born within these religious categories.

Then there are certain groups that claim that through a positive mental attitude and particular participation with the spirit world, one can attain a tremendous amount of wealth and material gain. These realms and groups are not part of the Holy Trinity, and the holy order and Christ are never mentioned. Anything that focuses on this particular mental attitude—actually, mind control participation back and forth, sometimes with the spirit world as well, concentrating on positive thinking and the pursuit of wealth—all of these actions become subject here to the lower pagan dominions. None of these are in the least associated with the Christian world of Christ and His sacred teachings. The light of the Holy Spirit is not present in these categories.

Judaism and its realms are powerful. The Jewish race are God's chosen people. The Judeo-Christian teachings are passed down through the centuries. However, when we read the Bible carefully, it is shown that Jesus in actuality went through His passion in order to draw all, including the Jews and those who are lost in their unbelief and others hanging on a thread, so to speak, into the holy presence of God.

In (Ephesians 2:15,16,17 & 18)*4:, it speaks especially about this important fact that Jesus' passion contained much to draw mankind to God.

> He abolished the Jewish Law with its commandments and rules, in order to create out of two races one new people in union with himself. In this way making peace. By his death on the cross, Christ destroyed their enmity; by means of the cross he united both races into one body and brought them back to God. So Christ came and preached the God News of peace to all, to you gentiles, who were far away from God, and to the Jews who were near to him. It is through Christ that all of us are able to come into one spirit into the presence of the Father.

The world can be an exciting place to live for those who anticipate new plans and ventures in this journey on earth; yet it is difficult and trying for those who are suffering due to debilitating and chronic illnesses. Whatever the case may be, no matter where life has brought an individual, the primary and most important fact is that there is a God and Creator; there is a Trinity that exists! It is not a delusion, figment of one's imagination, or merely some sort of crutch that some who are intellectually knowledgeable will try to ascertain.

Science can undoubtedly, according to some, negate and explain all kinds of phenomena. No, science and religion are coming closer together and will do so as time goes on, and they will disclose much. But when the elements and the wonderful mathematical equations in relation to this world are studied and understood more thoroughly and man ventures further into outer space, the Creator will become ever more profound. Such is the case when we seek deeper within ourselves and come to a closer union with God and Christ and His Trinity. We can then also come to an awareness of His holy presence and light.

This was the very essence of Christ's passion, and this was His passion! It was primarily to draw all and every man and woman into the presence of God. In doing so, He also gave those who were baptized the gifts of the Holy Spirit.

His passion is the Holy Eucharist—the Holy Communion that so graciously contains the light and love of God and that envelops all—sins, sorrows, direction, and healing. It is a time when we unite ourselves in the holy light, Holy Spirit, and passion of Christ. When we make our requests, they are heard and followed up, and we can continue and follow on a road that contains the light and leads us further into the holy light and love of God.

> With all your science, can you tell me
> How it is that Light comes into the Soul?
> —Henry David Thoreau

The Generational Healing Community

Directors: Rev Lloyd & Mrs Margaret Williams

24th May 2009

Ms Marianne Prins
P.O. Box 18
Mount Tabor
New Jersey
07878
USA

Dear Ms Prins

Your letter has been forwarded from our previous address in Hutton le Hole. Our current address is at the foot of this letter. I am sorry for the delay.

I heard of the Holy Communion offered for the slaves who perished in transportation across the Bermuda Triangle from several sources not least from Kenneth himself. We ministered alongside Dr Kenneth from the late 1980's right up until our time in Hong Kong and thereafter when we returned. We knew two or three of the people who were involved in the initial Holy Communion. It was conducted just a mile or so from our present home.

I often use the story when I meet those who are sceptical about the ministry, asking them 'When did you last hear of an incident in the Bermuda Triangle?' Of course their answer is and must be 'not since the late 1970's. I have not heard of a single incident since that time.

We are aware of many such stories not only in our own ministry but also in the ministry of several others where similar experiences have been known. For example places where road accidents have been common, reports of ghostly individuals distracting drivers' attention etc. These have been resolved following a Holy Communion being celebrated either for the casualties of earlier accidents or other events.

Other incidences where much blessing has followed a Holy Communion have concerned places with unresolved trauma either physical or spiritual.

We always minister in the context of a Holy Communion whether it be for places or individuals and have seen amazing miracles occur. When we lead a conference we always include teaching on the Communion. We have led many such conferences in Europe, Asia and the USA with amazing results from the Lord.

Our daughter lives in Northern British Columbia and so pass through Vancouver on occasion. We were invited to lead a conference in Calgary but this had to be cancelled when we discovered that it was to be held in a New Age centre.

I trust this helps.

With love and prayers in Christ Jesus

46 Royd Court, Mirfield, England WF14 9DJ
Telephone 44 (0) 1924 480898   E Mail revllovd@bsky.com   Web site healingtrust.info

About the Author

Ms. Prins had the opportunity to live in various areas such as Europe and the Far East due to the fact that her father was in the Diplomatic Service and an official of the State Department. Her family, having such a colorful life, also lived for some time on the premises of the Palace of Chulalongkorn, king of Thailand. She is a Eucharistic lay minister and attends both the Catholic Church and the Church of England. Being an artist as well, she exhibits her work frequently.

NOTES

Chapter 1   Hope and Wisdom

1. "Moments of Vision" by Kenneth Clark – Museum Director and Art Historian – Claredon Press, Oxford. U.K.
2. "Angels God's Secret Agents" by Billy Graham – DoubleDay & Co., Inc., Garden City, N.Y.

Chapter 2   The Inner Voice

"Making All Things New" by Henry J.M. Nouwen – Harper & Row Publishers.

Chapter 3 For He Will Give His Angels Charge Over Thee

1. Psalm 91

2. "Tramp for the Lord" by Corrie ten Boom – Fleming H. Revell Co.
3. "Man in White" by Johnny Cash – Harper Collins Publishers
4. "Angels God's Secret Agents" by Billy Graham – Double Day & Co., Garden City, N.Y.

Chapter 4 Dreams

"The Dream Source Book" by Amy Lenley and Phyllis R. Koch-Sheras Ph.D – Lowell House, Los Angeles, CA.

Chapter 5 I Go and Prepare a Place for You

1. "Behold Your God" by Agnes Sanford – Macalister Park Publishing Co. – St. Paul, Minnesota.
2. "Return from Tomorrow" by George C. Ritche, Jr. Kilmarnock, Virginia – a Classic Article from Guidepost, March 1989.

Chapter 6 Places of Interest

"Family Tree Ministry" issue November 1998 – Brochure #8 United Kingdom

Chapter 7 Star Wars

1. "Unmasking the Powers" by Walter Wink – Fortress Press, Philadelphia, PA.

2. "Creation Waits" by Agnes Sanford – Logos International, Publishers, Plainfield, N.J.

Chapter 8 God's Purpose

1. "Sealed Orders" by Agnes Sanford – Logos International Publishers, Plainfield, N.J.
2. "Beyond Ourselves" by Catherine Marshall – McGraw-Hill Co.
3. "Tramp for the Lord by Corrie ten Boom, Christian Literature Crusade – Fleming H. Revell, Old Tappan,NJ.

Chapter 9 Retreat

1. "Contemplating Now" by Monica Furlong – Cowley Publications – 28 Temple Place, Boston, Mass.
2. "Retreat Booklet" from the Franciscan Mission Associates, P.O.Box 598, Mt. Vernon, N.Y.

Chapter 10 Prayer

"The Divine Mercy" Marian Press, Stockbridge, Mass.

Chapter 11 The Holy Eucharist

1. "Miracles of the Eucharist" This is my body, This is My Blood. By Bob and Penny Lord, Publishers Journey of Faith – 1-800-633-2484.

2. "Healing the Family Tree" by Dr. Kenneth McAll, Sheldon Press, London, U.K.

Chapter 12 The Light

1. "The Healing Light" by Agnes Sanford, Arthur James Limited Publishers, The Drift, Evesham Worcs, UK
2. "Medjugorje Newsletter" December 2005, Weible Columns, 6814 Larkin Rd., Jacksonville, FL
3. "The 101 Times" #65, 101 Foundation, Box 151, Asbury, N.J.
4. Ephesians 2:15, 16, 17 & 18.
   Good News Bible – Catholic – Published by the American Bible Society – 1865 Broadway, New York 10023